the introvert's
guide to the
workplace

CONCRETE STRATEGIES FOR
BOSSES AND EMPLOYEES
TO THRIVE AND SUCCEED

Thea Orozco

Skyhorse Publishing

Skyhorse Publishing books may be purchased in bulk at special discounts for sales promotion, corporate gifts, fund-raising, or educational purposes. Special editions can also be created to specifications. For details, contact the Special Sales Department, Skyhorse Publishing, 307 West 36th Street, 11th Floor, New York, NY 10018 or info@skyhorsepublishing.com.

Skyhorse® and Skyhorse Publishing® are registered trademarks of Skyhorse Publishing, Inc.®, a Delaware corporation.

Visit our website at www.skyhorsepublishing.com.

10 9 8 7 6 5 4 3 2 1

Library of Congress Cataloging-in-Publication Data is available on file.
Library of Congress Control Number: 2020931631

Cover design by Daniel Brount

Print ISBN: 978-1-5107-5415-7
Ebook ISBN: 978-1-5107-5416-4

Printed in the United States of America

table of contents

INTRODUCTION

From entrepreneurs like Bill Gates to fashion designers like Eileen Fisher, athletes like Michael Jordan and film directors like Ang Lee, introverts can be found at the top of every field and industry. These celebrities haven't succeeded despite their introversion. Instead, their introvert strengths have helped them succeed. And you have those same introvert strengths.

Unfortunately, not every workplace is designed to help all employees thrive. Modern workplaces cater to gregarious extroverts, with noisy open-plan offices, brainstorming sessions, and mandatory (fun!) socializing with team-building exercises and holiday parties. A 2017 study found that in the workplace, "well-being is lower overall for individuals with a preference for Introversion (I) compared to those with a preference for Extraversion (E)."[1] This finding is probably no surprise to introverts living in an extrovert-biased society. You may have picked up, in subtle or overt ways, the message that our skills and natural talents aren't useful and that we need to dramatically change our personalities if we want to have a successful career.

This idea that we have to ignore or "overcome" our strengths to be happy at work is a myth.

This book was written to help introverts reconnect with the strengths and talents they've been taught to ignore. This is not a book that will try to turn you into an extrovert; instead, it acknowledges that most jobs require some form of "extroverting," and it provides tips and advice for those times when we need to step out of our "effortless zone." You'll also find that this book isn't about surface-level tips but rather about questioning what we've been told about ourselves and the ways we need to show up and behave.

When I first started blogging about introversion seven years ago, it was widely seen as a defect and mistakenly used as a synonym for shyness. There were only a handful of others talking about the quiet strengths of introversion—people like Andy Mort, Jenn Granneman, Jennifer Kahnweiler, Michaela Chung, and Brenda Knowles.

In 2012, Susan Cain's book *Quiet: The Power of Introverts in a World That Can't Stop Talking* became a *New York Times* bestseller, and the "introvert positive" movement expanded beyond a handful of bloggers. We're now in an age where the negative stereotypes of introverts are increasingly replaced by the acknowledgment of the strengths that introverts share. And while there are still plenty of people who use the word *shyness* and *introversion* interchangeably, on the whole, the conversation around introversion has changed considerably for the better.

This change is best summed up in an *Introverts Talking Business* podcast interview with Beth Buelow, who has been writing about introversion since 2010 under the brand the Introvert

Entrepreneur. Beth told me that when she first started her business, she set up a Google alert to inform her whenever a new article mentioning introversion was published. At first, she found that a large percentage of articles mentioning introversion were about criminals, and how the criminal in question was described as an "introvert and a loner." But now her Google alert is filled with articles about how we make great leaders, parents, and business owners. There have been so many introvert-positive articles published over the past five years that I've even seen articles written by extroverts complaining that introverts are getting all of the attention—which is quite the irony!

We are in a unique time in history to thrive in the workplace and to change the landscape of the office and the culture around us. Whether you are a boss or an employee, a career-oriented person, or someone who prioritizes other parts of your life, if you have to collaborate with colleagues, answer to bosses, and deal with clients, this book is for you. *The Introvert's Guide to the Workplace* will teach you how to use your natural introvert strengths to get ahead, as well as provide tips on how to survive those times when you need to "play the extrovert."

For the past seven years, I've been writing articles about introversion and running the social media accounts Introverts Everywhere and Introvertology, as well as talking about introversion in the podcast *Introverts Talking Business*. As a certified life coach, I've helped introverts navigate an extroverted society and thrive; as a business coach, I've shown introvert business owners how to tap into their innate introverted leadership skills; and as a consultant, I have helped businesses and nonprofits tap into the strengths of everyone on their teams, both introverts and extroverts. I'm excited to bring the knowledge I've gained over those many years to the page.

You *do* have what it takes to thrive in the workplace.

"In my customer service role, I use my intuition, patience, and ability to connect one-on-one. These are things that come so naturally, I do them without thinking about it. When I get compliments on 'how incredibly patient' I am, it reminds me that not everyone has these strengths that we tend to take for granted."

—Angelica, customer service representative

I.

WHAT IS INTROVERSION?

Quiet Revolutionary

Before he led a revolution, he was a shy law student. He had left home at the age of eighteen to study law in a foreign country, and now, three years later, he was back home in India. He knew little about the laws of his native country and struggled to understand its intricacies. However, his family had gone into debt to support his studies so he could get his law degree, so despite feeling like a fraud, he started looking for clients. He rented an office, put up his shingle, and waited . . . but very few cases came his way.

Finally, he was hired for an "easy case" that would only take up one day of his time. Representing the defendant, his main responsibility would be to cross-examine the plaintiff's witness.

And that's how Mahatma Gandhi found himself sitting nervously in a courtroom waiting for his first time to speak in the Small Causes Court. At last, the moment came for him to cross-examine the witness. Gandhi stood up—and froze. His mind went blank. He couldn't think of a single thing to ask the plaintiff's witness. In his autobiography *The Story of My Experiments with Truth*, he describes the courtroom as reeling around him. He imagined the judge was laughing at him, although the room was spinning too much for him to actually see if that was true. Unable to think or see straight, he sat down and then told his client's representative that he couldn't conduct the case.[2]

Gandhi's first court case was a resounding failure.

Not exactly the type of behavior one would expect from a person who would go on to launch multiple revolutions while leading a very public life of nonviolent protest. What changed? Was Gandhi's ability to shape the world through his leadership proof that he had stopped being a shy introvert and had turned into a talkative extrovert?

I don't think Gandhi transformed into an extrovert. I believe what changed for him and what enabled him to become a revolutionary leader was that he overcame his extreme shyness, which is to say he overcame the fear of negative judgment that had caused him so much anxiety. But Gandhi retained his introversion—his innate need to go inward for his energy—which helped him to think deeply about the world around him and to challenge what the culture he lived in considered to be the truth.

I Thought I Was Broken

While I'm no Gandhi, I was a shy and quiet child. Growing up in the United States, it was pretty clear to me that I didn't fit the American concept of "normal." Socially, I only had one good friend at a time and cycled through four best friends between the ages of six and fourteen. Academically, pretty much every report card of mine declared, "Does not speak up in class." Of course, there was also the occasional negative comment by peers, with one sixth-grade classmate turning to me out of the blue and saying, "It's always the quiet ones who turn out to be serial killers."

On top of that, in my early teens, I felt like I was failing at being a girl with regards to what I thought were things every girl should do. I hated talking on the phone, and I disliked going to the mall. Back then, I didn't have the words *introversion* or *HSP* (Highly Sensitive Person) in my vocabulary, but I knew I was different from the popular kids.

When I was fifteen, I subscribed to *Seventeen*, a magazine for teen girls. I read up on how to be normal. I bought jeans even though I disliked the coarse feeling of the material on my skin, I bleached my bangs and purchased a metal lunch box like the one I saw in the magazine. Unsurprisingly, at the end of the day, I didn't fool anyone, including myself, into thinking I was now "normal."

My "wait, I'm actually normal?!" moment didn't arrive until my early twenties when I picked up the book *The Introvert Advantage* by Marti Olsen Laney. It was life-changing.

Hold up, I thought. *I'm not broken?! And there's a biological reason why I act the way I do!*

I was also amazed to learn that shyness, which Laney described as "social anxiety, an extreme self-consciousness when one is around people," was not synonymous with introversion, which Laney described as the state of being "energized by the internal world." I was relieved to learn that although I had, for the most part, grown out of my childhood shyness and had become president of two clubs in college, I was still, at the core, my same introvert self.

Whereas *The Introvert Advantage* had felt like an older sister saying, "Hey, it's okay, there's nothing wrong with you," the next book I read on introversion, *Introvert Power* by Laurie Helgoe, was like having a big sister ready to fight the bullies who were saying I was broken. Not only that, Helgoe included an update to the often-cited statistic that originated in the 1950s—that introverts make up 25 percent of the population. She noted that a large-scale study in 1998 had actually found that 50.7 percent of the US population identified as introverts![3] While doing research for this book, I found that introverts are an even higher percentage of the global population. Using a global sample of over 16,000 people, the most recent MBTI® Manual published in 2018 reports that introverts make up 56.8 percent of the worldwide population![4]

Introverts are, literally, normal.

When I first looked into the Myers–Briggs Personality Types and learned that I was an INFJ (Introversion, Intuition, Feeling, Judgment), I was once again amazed to find that there were others like me. I was part of a group of people who tend to heavily weigh other people's feelings while making a decision and who constantly search for patterns in the world around them. But even as I realized that there are many people who are just as weird as I am, I also discovered introverts who are very different from me. While I tend to be anxious and reticent, other introverts are often brash and combative. My mind was blown.

When I graduated from college in 2003, Laney's book on introversion had just been published the year before, and there was very little advice on the internet about how to thrive as an introvert adult. Most of the career advice I came across seemed inapplicable, inauthentic, or pretty much impossible. I had no idea how to manage my anxiety at job interviews or how to navigate the social aspects of work, such as balancing requests from coworkers who asked me out to lunch with my need to spend that midday moment by myself to recharge.

What I needed was a manual.

We Weren't Given a Manual

I don't know about you, but on my first day at my very first job out of college, I wasn't given a manual titled, "How to thrive in the workplace as an introvert." In fact, it felt like I had been given a sticky note with the message: "Hopefully, you'll get by somehow despite your weirdness."

Well, this book *is* the manual I wish I had been given.

While not everyone wants to be a revolutionary leader like Gandhi, I think everyone wants to feel understood and respected at their job and to know that they are making a difference. But that can seem like an impossible dream for an introvert who still struggles with being misunderstood in general. As Susan Cain described in *Quiet*, over the past century, American culture moved from a "culture of character" to a "culture of personality."[5] As extroversion and the "culture of personality" became the ideal, introverts had to learn to act like extroverts in order to reach their goals. Having grown up in the United States, I assumed that all successful people were outgoing and charismatic. Even the people who managed to create a career where they marched to the beat of their own drum, like the singer Weird Al, seemed to exude an energy I could never match.

And although amazing writers like Susan Cain have helped to bring attention to the fact that introverts are not broken, we're still living in a culture that celebrates extroversion today. People often look at me as if I'm making things up when I say Elon Musk is an introvert, simply because they assume that success and fame are mutually exclusive with introversion.

In extrovert-focused societies like here in the United States, the label of introversion is still confused with shyness and seen as something that should be overcome so we can fit into the company culture. But there is power to being an introvert, and the word *introvert* should be embraced and used by our coworkers, our employers, and ourselves to highlight the natural gifts and talents we have that help us to uniquely excel in our jobs.

Unfortunately, many employers have designed workplaces that support extroverts but leave introverts feeling unheard and exhausted at the end of the day. From "team building exercises" that leave us feeling isolated, to brainstorming sessions where our voices aren't heard, to overwhelming open-plan offices, it's likely that the business or nonprofit where you work hasn't taken your way of being into consideration. This is a shame, since I believe it's possible for businesses to also cater to their introverted employees with just a few tweaks, which would allow them to tap into a spring of potential.

While we can't force people to accept us as we are, we introverts can make small (or big) changes to the way we show up at work that will increase our productivity and quality of life. And perhaps with that, we can ignite a change and create a worldwide culture that provides a space for everyone to flourish.

Introversion Is . . .

I would love to share with you the single definition of introversion that everyone agrees on . . . unfortunately, it doesn't exist. Ask any two people to define introversion, and they will probably give you two different answers. One might say that introverts are shy; another might say that they're overwhelmed by large groups of people.

I've found that most interpretations of introversion can be grouped into four main concepts:

1. Introverts are shy.
2. Introverts get overstimulated more quickly than extroverts.
3. Introverts are less motivated by seeking rewards.
4. Introverts gain energy by being alone.

Your coworkers and bosses are likely subscribing to one of these definitions, which will in turn affect how they treat you. Let's examine each of these definitions.

1. Introverts are shy.

A widespread definition of introverts is that they are shy. Do not use this definition, please, I beg you. It is a myth and misconception.

To recap, shyness, as Marti Olsen Laney described in *The Introvert Advantage*, is "an extreme self-consciousness when one is around people."[6] While many, but certainly not all, introverts are self-conscious around others, many extroverts are

9

self-conscious around other people, too. Simply, shyness is not a defining attribute of introversion. We'll speak more about the difference between introversion and shyness later on in this chapter.

2. Introverts get overstimulated more quickly than extroverts.

Another common definition is how easily introverts become overstimulated. One of the pioneers of this concept was the psychologist Hans Eysenck. According to his theory, "extroverts tend to exhibit lower levels of ascending reticular activating system activity as compared to that of the introverts."[7] The Ascending Reticular Activating System (ARAS), a network of nerves located in the brainstem, regulates wakefulness and vigilance. In other words, it is much easier for introverts to become overwhelmed because we already have a lot of activity going on in our brains. If you've ever walked into a noisy bar and your brain shuts down suddenly while your extroverted friend seems right at home, you've seen this in action.

This definition seems to have decreased in popularity among personality researchers, but it's still used in articles and books about personality traits.

3. Introverts are less motivated by the act of seeking rewards.

Imagine yourself on a calm, relaxing beach. Seems like a nice place to be, right? Now imagine yourself buying a lottery ticket and then winning a week's worth of wages! Exciting, right? While relaxing on a beach is pleasant, money is exciting. Like food and social status, money falls under what scientists refer to as a "reward," a strong external incentive. The act of buying a lottery ticket, in hopes of winning money, means you're pursuing a possible exciting reward!

Researchers Smillie, Cooper, Wilt, and Revelle asked introverts and extroverts to imagine a number of situations, some merely pleasant, and others involving the pursuit of a possible reward. After imagining themselves buying a lottery ticket and winning £1000 instantly, extroverted participants reported feeling higher levels of "*enthusiastic, excited, elated, peppy, euphoric,* and *lively*" emotions than introverts. But when it came to imagining themselves relaxing on the beach, introverts and extroverts felt similarly happy.[8] Their research showed that introverts are less motivated than extroverts by the act of seeking rewards.

This difference between what introverts and extroverts feel when they imagine the pursuit of a reward is due to the chemical in the brain called dopamine. In *The Secret Lives of Introverts: Inside Our Hidden World,* author Jenn Granneman writes, "Dopamine itself doesn't guarantee that you'll feel pleasure. What is does guarantee is you'll be excited by the *possibility* of pleasure. In a restaurant, when a server shows you a tray of tantalizing desserts and you get excited about eating one, that's dopamine at work."[9]

This could explain why your extroverted friend would love to go out and meet new people (social status is a "reward"), but you're content with finishing that novel you started yesterday; you're just not as excited by the possibility of the reward. An extrovert once told me that he got himself through a very boring meeting at the end of a workday by doodling an image of a cocktail on a pad of paper. He was motivating himself to get through the meeting by anticipating not just the external reward of an alcoholic drink, but also the external reward of hanging out and socializing with other people! I, on the other hand, often amuse myself during boring meetings by thinking of lists—what I need to buy at the grocery store, my favorite Doctor Who companions, etc. In other words, during a boring meeting, I tend to either occupy myself with random thoughts or productive lists, versus an extrovert who might try to keep their energy levels up by thinking about external rewards.

While introverts do sometimes enjoy pursuing external rewards, we tend to just not be as excited by it as extroverts. And because we're less excited about pursuing external rewards, we often don't think about them as much, and, therefore, we are less driven by the idea of rewards.

4. Introverts gain energy by being alone.

For the past seven years that I've been running online communities as a life and business coach for introverts, I have seen a significant shift in perception about introversion. Many extroverts, and even many introverts, used to define introversion as shyness, which is an easy mistake to make. Today, most of the introverts I come across define an introvert as a person who recharges their energy by being alone and who has their energy drained when they socialize with others.

When I reached out to my Twitter followers to ask for their definitions of introversion, a few of them responded:

> "People who require space, quiet, and time to think about answers to questions and problems, or even to do their jobs; and who get emotionally and physically exhausted when forced into loud, busy, crowded environments for hours."

"Time spent with others = energy given out. Time spent alone = recharge time!"

"Quiet time to think = a natural, effortless state; noisy time in social activities = continuous conscious effort."

"Powered from within."

While two of these answers mention the element of thinking and the other two do not, all four define introversion in terms of energy. This definition is loosely based on the theories of the Swiss psychologist Carl Jung who popularized the terms *introversion* and *extraversion* (the original spelling of *extroversion*) in the psychological sense in the 1920s. Jung's theory, which we'll discuss later, formed the basis of the well-known personality indicator, the Myers–Briggs Type Indicator (MBTI).

I find that most introverts relate to this energy-based definition the best. I'll be using this fourth definition of introversion throughout this book.

Tips for Managing Introverts

Are you a leader or manager in the workplace? Do you have a definition of introversion that matches one of the definitions in this chapter? Creating definitions and mental shortcuts about a segment of the population, even one you might belong to, can quickly turn into pigeonholing and stereotyping, which ultimately does a disservice to the employee. In reality, we're all individuals.

Here are a few questions you can ask yourself to start uncovering your assumptions about introverts:

- How do I define introversion?
- When someone tells me they are an introvert, what is my reaction?
- How do I expect an introvert to act?
- How have introverts I've interacted with in the past behaved?
- How do the introverts I've interacted with behave differently from one another?

Once you identify your expectations and question your assumptions, it's much easier to see the introvert in front of you for who they truly are.

Am I an Introvert?

If you aren't sure what side of the introvert–extrovert spectrum you swing, let me ask you one question:

It's a Friday, and it's been a very long week at work. You've put in a lot of hours and are exhausted. What do you want to do next—go home, or go out?

Of course, if you answered, "go home," you're most likely an introvert! But if your idea of starting a relaxing weekend is being around other people, you're most probably an extrovert. If your answer depends on your mood, you may be an ambivert, someone in the middle of the spectrum. Look for tendencies and patterns in the way you recharge your energy to find out if you're an introvert or an extrovert.

Still not sure if you're an introvert? Here are a few characteristics many introverts relate to:

- Dislikes small talk
- Likes nature
- Enjoys working independently rather than taking part in group projects
- Gets really excited and talkative when speaking about something they love but can struggle to be engaged in conversations they are not interested in
- Has trouble formulating on-the-spot answers to questions
- Experiences sensory overload, such as getting uncomfortable or overwhelmed after experiencing too many sights, sounds, etc. (If this describes you, you may also be a Highly Sensitive Person on top of being an introvert.)
- "Shuts down" or gets grumpy after prolonged social interaction
- Dislikes open-plan offices
- Focuses on work instead of engaging in chitchat with coworkers
- Has a few close friends
- Dislikes parties
- Prefers texting or emailing to speaking on the phone

Don't worry if only a few of these describe you; introverts come in all different shapes and sizes. You'll still be able to pick up tips and tricks from this book to help you thrive in the workplace.

The Different Faces of Introversion

I'm an introvert, and so is my very good friend Lisa Avebury, who has a worldwide touring company called Sacred Introvert Retreat Tours. But we're very different people. I'm a homebody, while she likes going to gardens and museums and estate sales. I generally don't talk to strangers, but she'll walk up to someone and tell them she likes their hat. I'm active on social media, but she stays off it as much as possible.

This breadth of differences among introverts and among theories of introversion has been noted by many psychologists in the past, and it led psychologists Jennifer O. Grimes, Jonathan Cheek, Julie K. Norem, and Courtney A. Brown to examine those wide-ranging differences. They designed a survey combining nineteen different scales designed to measure introversion/extraversion and administered it to 225 female students. The end result culminated in the theory that there are four types of introversion—Social, Thinking, Anxious, and Restrained, resulting in the mnemonic STAR. An introvert can score high or low on each of these traits.[10]

Do you identify with one or more of the following types of introverts?

Social introverts value their alone time and prefer smaller groups of people to larger groups.

Thinking introverts are pensive daydreamers. They have an inclination toward self-reflection and introspection.

Anxious introverts are self-conscious in social situations. They are also anxious at home and ruminate on events they would rather forget.

Restrained introverts can take a while to wake up in the morning. They prefer to take things easy and think something through before speaking.[11]

What I like about this theory is that it shows there is no one right way to be an introvert—or even one right way to be a human being.

Personality Theories through Time

The social practice of forcing people into boxes began a very long time ago, and some ancient theories of personality still affect us and how we lead our lives today.

Barring access to a time machine/TARDIS, we may never know what the first multifaceted theory of personality looked like. Still, we do know that personality theories are older than recorded history.

Ayurveda, a medical system originating in India, was first recorded roughly five thousand years ago in the Indus valley,[12] around the same time that writing was invented. And judging from the complexity of the theory, it most likely had a long oral history before it was written down. In India, around 70 percent of its rural population still practice the Ayurvedic system of medicine today.[13] According to Ayurveda, all of life, including the human body, consists of five natural elements—fire, water, earth, air, and ether (space).[14] The combinations of these five elements govern various functions of a human being's physical, emotional, and mental characteristics. We're all born with varying degrees of these elements, and illnesses arise when our own personal combination of elements becomes greatly imbalanced. Imbalances are often due to environmental factors, such as the type of food you eat. So, by eating the right foods, for example, we can find our internal balance again.

Fast forward three thousand years to the second century, around 150 CE, when the Greek physician Galen, personal physician to several Roman emperors, devised his own explanation of behavior and health. During his medical training, Galen was most likely instructed in the medical theories of the Greek physician Hippocrates. Hippocrates theorized that the human body contains four fluids (blood, "yellow bile," phlegm, and "black bile"), which need to be balanced in order to achieve physical health (sound familiar?). Galen expanded this theory to also explain differences in personality. According to Galen's theory, if you're passionate and bossy, you would be described as *Choleric* and would have an excess of the fluid yellow bile. If you are confident and high-energy, you would be referred to as *Sanguine* and have a surplus of blood in your system. *Melancholic* people, with an excess of black bile, are sensitive and pensive. Meanwhile, *Phlegmatic* people, who have an excess of phlegm, would be peaceful and unexcitable.[15]

Did you notice anything about those descriptions? Don't Choleric and Sanguine people sound like stereotypes of an extrovert, while Melancholic and Phlegmatic people sound like stereotypes of an introvert? Surprisingly, Galen's concept of the four temperaments was popular in certain cultures up until the 1700s! Occasionally, I still hear someone described as being choleric or sanguine.

The next famous theory I'd like to discuss was created by Carl Jung in the 1920s. Jung popularized *introversion* and *extraversion* as psychology terms—an introvert is a person who is primarily turned inward toward their own thoughts and ideas, while extraverts are directed outward to things outside the self. Jung's theory struck a chord with the public, so much so that in 1957, Dr. Richard Evens, while interviewing Jung, noted: "These terms have now become so widely known that the man on the street is using them constantly in describing members of his family, his friends, and so on. They have become probably the psychological concepts most often used by the layman today."[16] Today, nearly one hundred years later, we're still using the terms *introvert* and *extrovert* to describe aspects of a person's personality! And modern research has been hard at work, trying to understand what it means to be an introvert or extrovert.

The theory of personality used by most personality psychologists today is called "The Big Five." The Big Five posits that there are five main aspects to a person's personality, which can be memorized using the acronym OCEAN: Openness, Conscientiousness, Extroversion, Agreeableness, and Neuroticism. How does the Big Five describe introversion? Well, it doesn't. There are extroverts, and then there are people who just score low on extroversion. The influential researchers and personality psychologists Robert McCrae and Paul Costa describe extroversion as having the facets of warmth, gregariousness, assertiveness, activity, excitement seeking, and positive emotions.[17] I know many introverts who would really dislike being regarded as someone who lacks warmth and assertiveness and who would say that the Big Five description isn't entirely accurate. I also object to the idea that introverts are just "low on extroversion." Nevertheless, the Big Five is the prevailing description of personality used by personality psychologists.

It's in Your Brain

To learn how to thrive as an introvert in the workplace, we first need to figure out what it means to be authentic and true to your introverted self. While individual pieces of research can't definitively give us answers, they can be puzzle pieces in the bigger picture of how to succeed in the world and at work.

Fortunately, technology today is allowing us to scan people's brain structure and examine their brain chemicals. We are getting closer to understanding the biological source of differences in personality.

In her book *The Introvert Advantage*, Marti Olsen Laney discussed a study by Dr. Debra Johnson that examined the difference between what's going on in an introvert's and an extrovert's brain while resting in a positron emission tomography (PET) scanner. Laney describes that for introverts, "blood flowed to the parts of the brain involved with internal experiences like remembering, solving problems, and planning." For extroverts, blood flowed "to the areas of the brain where visual, auditory, touch, and taste (excluding smell) sensory processing occurs." Even while resting in a PET scanner, introverts and extroverts have different ways of being! This research shows that we are natural planners. Planning can be used as a source of strength for introverts, and throughout this book, you'll read about how to make use of this strength in all areas of the workplace—from speaking up in meetings to networking.

One of my favorite studies on the differences between introverts and extroverts involves the drug Ritalin, which is often prescribed to people with ADHD because it helps with concentration. In 2013, Cornell University scientists Richard A. Depue and Yu Fu administered Ritalin to research participants, then proceeded to show them a few videos, several of which would typically be considered boring. Because of the drug, subjects found those "boring" videos interesting. After the drug wore off, subjects were shown the videos again, in the same room they had originally watched the films. There was a difference in how introverts and extroverts responded! Even though they were no longer under the effects of the drug, the extroverts who had been given Ritalin became excited because they associated the room with the positive feelings they had felt when they first watched the movie. However, introverts, and the control group of extroverts who had never been given the drug, couldn't care less about being in that room and rewatching the same boring videos. Richard Depue, one of the researchers of the study, describes its findings in this way: "Extroverts will acquire a more extensive network of reward-context memories that activate their brain's reward system."[18] Have you ever had a pretty good time at a party or networking event but find that you still have to force yourself to leave the house to attend similar types of events in the future? If so, you've experienced what this study described. I'll include tips in later chapters on how to motivate yourself to go to things like networking events or holiday parties—if that's something that aligns with your goals.

Now that we have a better idea of what introversion is, let's talk about what it's not.

Introvert Myths

I've come across six main myths about introversion:

1. We're all shy.
2. We aren't leaders.
3. We can't do public speaking.
4. We hate people.
5. We lack self-esteem.
6. We're aloof.

Let's examine each of these myths individually.

1. Introverts are shy.

Peter claimed he was no longer an introvert.

"Okay," I said, while wondering to myself why he had come to the event I had organized for introverts.

Peter proceeded to tell me that he used to stay silent whenever he was among a group of people, but that was in the past. Now, he could talk confidently in a group. What Peter thinks of as introversion, I think of as shyness. I often come across people, like Peter, who tell me mistakenly that they "used to be introverts but are now extroverts." After some probing, it almost always turns out that they simply outgrew their shyness and can now talk to people with ease. It's not unusual for someone to "grow" out of shyness. On the other hand, there's quite a bit of research suggesting that a decent amount of introversion is genetically determined.

A study from the University of Minnesota looked at 402 pairs of twins, including identical and fraternal twins, as well as twins who were raised together and apart. It concluded that when it comes to certain aspects of personality, "on average, about 50 percent of measured personality diversity can be attributed to genetic diversity." The researchers also concluded that the "overall contribution of a common family-environment component was small and negligible."[19]

In other words, it's likely that what had changed in Peter wasn't his temperament, an ingrained part of his personality, but rather a certain aspect of his outward behavior—his shyness.

Because of this long-standing myth that all introverts are shy, many people seem to think that if we introverts could just get over our supposed fear of socializing, we would turn out to be loud, exuberant extroverts and start hosting raucous parties. Umm, no.

In my case, it isn't fear that's preventing me from hosting raucous parties; it's my complete lack of interest in being involved in a loud party, or pretty much any party.

The reason this is such a long-standing myth is that from the outside, introversion and shyness may look indistinguishable from one another. If a shy person and an introvert walk into a noisy nightclub full of strangers, they're both going to look very unhappy. But they'll look unhappy for different reasons. Shyness stems from the fear of being judged—a shy person is going to worry about fitting in with everyone in that club. Meanwhile, an introvert who is not shy may look grumpy because they have hit their "introvert overwhelm" limit.

While there are definitely shy introverts in the world, there are also shy extroverts, too. In the book *Quiet*, Susan Cain explains that a shy extrovert like Barbra Streisand can have a big personality and also have extreme stage fright. Meanwhile, a non-shy introvert may behave like Bill Gates, who supposedly "keeps to himself but is unfazed by the opinions of others."[20]

Let's think about a hypothetical situation where Jackie, Mickey, and Rose are in the break room at work. Jackie tells Mickey, a shy extrovert, and Rose, a non-shy introvert, that she has tickets for an "awesome" singles party happening this weekend. Unfortunately, she can't go, and asks if either of them want her ticket—both refuse. Externally, the shy extrovert and non-shy introvert have the same reaction, refusing the free ticket. However, the internal reasons are very different. Mickey, the shy extrovert, might be thinking, "Ugh. I kind of want to go. But I'm not going to know anyone there. It's just going to be awkward." Meanwhile, Rose, the non-shy introvert, might be thinking,

"Ugh. That sounds exhausting!" Without knowing their underlying reasoning, Jackie might interpret Rose's response as proof that she is shy, and Jackie might think that Mickey is an introvert! What Jackie may not realize is that it's not a fear of awkwardness that is preventing Rose from attending, but rather the expectation of being exhausted and drained by an unfulfilling evening. Recall that current research is now saying that introverts just aren't as excited as extroverts when anticipating rewards.

In Chapter III, I'll revisit this concept that people often wrongly interpret our internal motivations based on specific external behaviors. I think it's crucial to remember that our managers and coworkers are often trying to guess our inner motivations by our external actions, and there is a possibility they might get it wrong.

2. Introverts can't be leaders.

Related to the toxic belief that all introverts are shy, it's also believed that we don't have what it takes to become leaders in the workplace.

I've had worried parents reach out to me because they're concerned about their introverted teenager's future, not understanding that introverts are just as capable as extroverts in achieving anything they set themselves to. We may have to work a little harder to overcome the introverts-are-shy bias, but ultimately introversion will not hold you back from becoming a leader if that's part of your career path. In fact, research studies suggest that introverts may even be better leaders than extroverts—more on that in another chapter.

3. Introverts can't do public speaking.

Once again, because of the toxic belief that all introverts are shy, there is also the mistaken belief that introverts cannot become good public speakers.

> ## Our strength of listening and connecting one-on-one with others can help us be amazing public speakers.

A study by the University of New Mexico compared the personality traits of comedians with college students and found that comedians were less extroverted than the typical student.[21] You don't have to be an extrovert to command a room. In another chapter, we'll discuss how you can become a better speaker—if that's important to you or your career.

4. Introverts hate people.

Over the past few years, I have talked to countless "people person" introverts—the truth is, they exist! Personally, I also like people, just in small doses. I've also met plenty of introverts who are friendly and socially adept but who are ambivalent about being social. And while there are some introverts who have learned to "hate people" (maybe being told that they were broken when they were growing up has something to do with that), in my experience, hating people is just not how the vast majority of introverts feel. Unfortunately, many people don't understand that introverts simply need to be alone to recharge. We don't seek out moments of solitude because we hate company or think we're too good to talk to other people; instead, when we are overwhelmed, we need our alone time in order to return to our energized "true" selves.

5. Introverts lack self-esteem.

Introverts are not born lacking self-esteem; there are plenty of introverts who are full of themselves. Unfortunately, many introverts, especially those who have grown up in an extrovert-focused society and/or who are particularly sensitive and empathic, have internalized the false story that there is something wrong with them. This belief that our innate introversion is wrong can lead to low self-esteem. I'm looking forward to the day when introvert children will grow up feeling that it's okay to be themselves. If this false narrative about introversion has affected you, know that you have the freedom to break out of that cycle of low self-esteem and shame and rewrite your story! I hope this book will help you realize that we do have strengths, and that if other introverts can break out of that cycle, you can, too.

6. Introverts are aloof.

Supposedly, introverts lack self-esteem; but we're also perceived as aloof and are told we think we're too good to talk to other people! Although stereotypes don't always make sense, they can still affect how someone is seen and treated by others.

In college, I was called aloof by a good friend. It threw me off at the time because I was used to being called "shy but friendly," and I thought I was a people-pleaser. But upon reflection, I understood why my friend had that impression even if it didn't match with my own self-image. I'm an independent person, prone to observing the things around me. While I'm usually a people-pleaser, I do have strict boundaries regarding certain issues, as well as a deep need to safeguard my independence. So when non-negotiable subjects or events come up, I won't budge.

In an extrovert-focused society where there's the saying "Strangers are just friends you haven't met yet," a person who communicates boundaries can be mistaken as being remote, stuffy, and aloof toward others. Extroverts in the workplace often don't understand that an introvert who chooses to eat lunch alone is not trying to be distant or unfriendly; rather, they are simply treasuring their alone-time and are trying to cope in an office environment that wasn't designed to increase their productivity or comfort.

Highly Sensitive People (HSP)

In addition to the myths above, another concept that often gets conflated with introversion is the highly sensitive person.

Many years ago, I went to the cinema to catch a screening of Steven Spielberg's *Saving Private Ryan*, a film about World War II. An intense battle scene came on screen, and after about two minutes of watching actors pretend to be blown apart, I became lightheaded, and spots appeared in my vision. I didn't think I could get up without falling down, so I put my head between my knees and hoped I had done enough to prevent me from fainting. Fortunately, it was enough.

I've always been "sensitive," so why I thought I could handle watching a violent war movie, I don't know. I've now wised up and have become very selective about what movies and TV shows I consume, choosing to stay away from violence or gore. But not every introvert is like this. My friend Rick, a fellow introvert, is obsessed with TV show *Game of Thrones* and has tried to convince me to watch it on multiple occasions. I have heard enough about the show to know that I will not find it fun to watch; it'll more likely be faint-inducing! Although Rick and I are similar in many ways, I'm an HSP and he's not.

Highly Sensitive Person (HSP) is a term coined by Elaine Aron, author of the aptly named book *The Highly Sensitive Person.* In her book, Aron describes the four aspects of high sensitivity:

Depth of processing: HSPs process everything deeply, which means they observe (gather information) before they act.

Overstimulated easily: Because they process things deeply, when the environment around them gets to be too much, they can easily become overstimulated.

Emotional responsiveness: According to Aron, "HSPs react more to both positive and negative experiences." They also have a stronger sense of empathy.

Subtle stimuli: HSPs are good at noticing the little details. This doesn't mean that they have better eyesight or hearing, but the way their brains process the stimuli means they pick up on subtleties more easily.[22]

In other words, if you observe before you act, get easily overwhelmed, dislike violent movies, and notice whenever someone gets a new haircut, you might be a Highly Sensitive Person. From the outside, HSPs and introverts can be confused for one another, but in fact, 30 percent of HSPs are extroverts.[23]

To explore the difference between HSPs, extroversion, and shyness, let's think about a situation where four people are driving in a car. An extrovert, who isn't shy or an HSP, might say, "Hey, I love that bar we just passed! We've only done boring stuff today. Let's go in!" Here are the reactions (spoken or unspoken) from everyone else in that car:

Shy non-HSP extrovert: Okay, but you won't all go dancing and leave me alone at the table, right?

HSP introvert: If you really want to, but I'm getting tired.

Non-shy HSP extrovert: Let's go! I still want to hear about your new girlfriend! Wait, is it one of those super loud bars? I don't think I can do a loud bar right now.

Particular aspects of the modern work environment can hamper an HSP's productivity. Although probably the vast majority of introverts find open-plan offices unpleasant, HSPs may find open-plan offices particularly distressing and inefficient places to work. For instance, the loud overheard conversations of coworkers can make it very hard for an HSP to focus on their work since they are usually hyper-aware of what's happening around them. Even something as simple as a printer suddenly turning on and printing a document can be enough to distract an HSP.

Although HSP introverts have their own set of challenges, they can, of course, be an integral part of the workplace. For instance, because HSPs easily pick up on other people's emotions, they may be the person colleagues come to when they need to talk about a problem. Since they're sensitive to subtle stimuli, they may also be the first to spot a problem in a product or process.

Throughout written history, humans have theorized that people are biologically different, and modern personality research has confirmed this theory. Introverts are not shy extroverts; introverts are introverts, and we make up more than half of the worldwide population. And yet from the outside, it can appear that we're far outnumbered because many introverts living in an extrovert-biased culture have learned to blend in. But introversion isn't a type of shyness that needs to be overcome. Introversion is genetic; it's part of who we are. And it doesn't matter how many myths about introversion exist; the truth is that we have plenty of gifts and strengths. In the next chapter, let's explore a few of those strengths and how you can use them in the workplace.

"As a lawyer, the most important and difficult skill is listening to your client, with full attention. Introverts do this better than extroverts."

—Gwen, lawyer

II.

AN INTROVERT'S INNER STRENGTHS

Your Strengths Are Real

In my sixth-grade class, we were instructed to write a report on any animal of our choosing. I chose the pufferfish, which, now that I think about it, is a very "leave me alone if I don't want to be bothered" type of fish. To research our animal, we were told to look through the *National Geographic* magazines that filled two very long bookshelves in the back of the classroom. Like the other kids, I started looking for articles on my chosen animal. And then I kept looking. And kept looking. I wanted to make sure that I was thorough, that I had found everything in those magazines about the pufferfish that I could find. I was still there, at the back of the class, researching, ten minutes after all the other students had left.

While I sat there and flipped through the magazines, in isolation while the rest of my classmates had moved on, a growing sense of unease started to form. Once again, I felt like I was the weird one. Eventually, my teacher, Miss Allen, came over to see what I was doing. I expected her to tell me that I should have stopped looking through the magazines long ago, but I was surprised when she turned to me and said, "Hey, you're good at research."

You may not have had a Miss Allen at school, someone who pointed out the positives of your personality. It's very likely that you don't have a Miss Allen at work, someone who will stop, look you in the eye, and say, "Hey, I see you—I recognize your talents and what you're drawn to." If you don't, *I* want to tell you that you do have strengths and gifts and talents. Some of your strengths are innate, some are learned. Some you will share with many other introverts. All of your strengths combine to create your square-peg advantage—your unique combination of strengths.

> ## If others don't acknowledge your strengths, that doesn't make them any less real.

In this chapter we'll be discussing your inner strengths so you can use your square-peg advantage to reach your workplace goals.

Tips for Managing Introverts

Each person has a *square-peg advantage*—strengths that come together to create a uniquely talented person.

However, a manager's preconceived notions about how a report should complete a task, or a manager's desire to follow the strict procedures and processes already in place, can prevent an introverted report from using their square-peg advantage, ultimately leading to a decrease in productivity and performance.

Here are a few questions you can ask yourself to uncover your report's square-peg advantage:

1. How does this person stand apart from other reports?
2. In which tasks does this person excel?
3. What does this person do that surprises me?
4. What does this person do that disappoints me?
5. Which policies and procedures does this person struggle with?

Noticing where a report falls short can sometimes point you in the direction of their strengths. Do they struggle with details? Consider assigning them to a project involving more strategy and big-picture thinking. Do they struggle with following policies or procedures? Try giving them a project with more creativity.

If an introvert struggles to "participate" in meetings (this is code for *speaking*), it may be that they are busy listening, and you may find they have a better grasp on what happened during the meeting than the other people present. How can you take advantage of your report's square-peg advantage?

Our Top Three Strengths

Introverts have many strengths, and I believe our top three are:

1. Our energy is created internally.
2. We think before acting.
3. We have superior listening skills.

1. Our Energy Is Created Internally.

Brené Brown is a research professor, bestselling author, and international speaker. You may have watched her TED talk "The Power of Vulnerability," which has so far gained more than forty-three million views. One of her talks was even taped and turned into a Netflix special. Because she's a professional speaker, she must be an extrovert and must crave being in the center of attention, right? Nope! Brené is an introvert. Less than three minutes into her Netflix special, she asks, "How many of you know I'm super introverted?" Although Brené does public speaking because it's a personal project of hers (more on the concept of personal projects later in another chapter), at the end of the day, she recharges by being in a low-stimulation environment and gathers her energy internally.

Gary Vaynerchuk is an entrepreneur, speaker, investor, and social media influencer. Like Brené Brown, Gary is accomplished in his field, and unlike Brené, he is very much an extrovert. He typically records his Q&A video series, #AskGaryVee, inside a meeting room with a handful of employees, but once, he filmed an episode outdoors in a crowded square. In the video, Gary was obviously thrilled with this change of scenery and talked about how he was energized by being around so many people. On the other hand, if it had been me out there doing the Q&A, my introversion might have caused me to be distracted by the new environment. I would have been too flustered by my surroundings to properly concentrate on the question I was trying to answer.

Whether you gain your energy from quiet places like Brené Brown or from busy environments like Gary Vaynerchuk, understand that both ways of gaining energy can be used as unique strengths in the workplace. Extroverts gain energy from interacting with the outside world, and since introverts don't need to seek points of contact with other people in order to recharge, we're pretty good at keeping our heads down and doing the work that's in front of us. Sometimes, that's what really matters in a job. In creative fields, our willingness to go inward also makes it easier for us to tap into unique thoughts.

Understanding our energy can also help us cope with the social aspects of life and work. If we think of our energy as a battery, then when our energy is filled, we have the luxury of listening fully to others with the energy we've stored up. If we learn to manage our energy and not let the necessary social interactions at our jobs drain us until we have an empty battery, then we can strategically connect with people in our workplace in an authentic way. Because you don't need other people to fill your energy tank, you can come to a conversation focused on *them* and *their* needs, rather than on *your* energy needs. Showing up to conversations with managers ready and prepared to help solve their problems can be a powerful way to make yourself indispensable at work.

2. We Think Before Acting.

Our first impulse is to think through things first. As a result, introverts are often seen as self-starters compared to colleagues who may pepper the boss or colleagues with questions. A compliment

I frequently get at work is that I just figure things out myself and save my boss a lot of time. Being a self-starter who thinks things through and just gets them done can be a huge asset when you have a poorly trained manager, or if you work in a fast-growing company where your manager may be juggling multiple roles and has to take a hands-off approach to management.

3. We Have Superior Listening Skills.

Listening, an innate introvert gift, is powerful, and it goes a long way to making the people around you feel heard.

Has this ever happened to you? You're speaking to someone, and you can see in their eyes that you aren't being heard. Perhaps they're lost in their own thoughts (more common in introverts) or just waiting for their turn to talk (more common in extroverts). How did not being heard make you feel? You probably felt frustrated, angered, insignificant, or unloved.

My friend Lisa Avebury, a fellow introvert, is an amazing listener. She once texted me to ask about something I didn't remember telling her. I was shocked that she had not only listened to me but had also remembered! It made me feel appreciated. The fact that I still remember her text a few years later is a testament to how infrequently I feel genuinely heard.

> ## Listening *is* a strength in the workplace.

Listening deeply is a powerful asset. It can create a bond between coworkers, and listening can be crucial to the effectiveness of many meetings. Your boss wants to know that you've understood her instructions, and you can do that through careful listening. Plus, in customer-facing or sales roles, it's very possible that listening is the most important factor in your success. In a later chapter, I'll introduce you to an introvert who used her skill of listening to become a top-performing salesperson.

Fortunately, being able to listen and being able to speak with ease are not mutually exclusive. Just as many extroverts can be naturally great at listening, or can learn to be great, many introverts are naturally great at conversing, or can learn to be confident in conversations or when speaking in public.

The Tendency to Treat Our Listening Strength as a Weakness

Being an introvert in an extroverted culture may affect the way we see our strengths. If you live in such an environment, you may have developed a dislike for your strength of listening, even interpreting the phrase "you're such a good listener" as an insult. Because extrovert-focused cultures often equate talking with intelligence and teach us that it's better to be chatty than pensive, some introverts have been socialized to forget our innate skill and the art of listening.

When society convinces us that our strengths are actually our weaknesses and forces us to overcompensate, we end up taking the erroneous concept of "talking = connecting" to the extreme. I've seen many introverts forget how to use this natural strength and flounder at networking events or completely talk over another person in a conversation. Through all my years of working with introverts, I've realized that not all nonstop talkers are extroverts. Though it sounds counterintuitive, I've noticed that if I'm trying to have a conversation with someone who is talking nonstop, and they seem anxious and unhappy, it's very possible they are an "anxious introvert," one of Grimes, et al.'s four categories of introverts that were discussed in Chapter I. I recently shared this observation on Facebook, and an acquaintance, let's call her Marla, confessed that she was an introvert who nervously talked nonstop.

I asked Marla what causes her to want to fill silence with speech, and she commented, "I try to be the person to keep the conversation going, and I keep filling up the space when I'm with people because I'm afraid of the awkward silence. I guess that I unconsciously don't want others to think I am boring or unsociable."

I can understand her reasoning. Marla lives in an extrovert society where gregariousness is rewarded and reticence is looked down upon. She was probably taught that silence (and introversion) was a weakness, so she learned to adapt by talking . . . a lot. Since she mentioned that she's afraid of awkward silences, she might also be a shy introvert, which probably compounds her anxiety.

Perhaps there were people in your early life—your family, or friends, or teachers—who taught you that "silence = weakness." They were wrong. Most people, even extroverts, subconsciously understand that silence does not mean you are weak. In fact, a study from the University of Michigan examined the relationship between speech patterns and persuasiveness and found that when trying to convince someone to take a telephone survey, the interviewers who spoke with no pauses convinced fewer people to take part in the survey compared to the interviewers who talked with long pauses between words. It was theorized that the fast talkers seemed less genuine.[24]

Whether you constantly raised your hand at school or would always get the end-of-year note "Does not speak up in class" (like me), please remember that listening is a strength. Trust me, when push comes to shove, your coworkers or boss will want someone there who can really listen to them.

Every Strength Is a Weakness and Every Weakness Is a Strength

Countless introverts have told me that they're jealous of an extrovert's ability to talk to just about anyone and of their seemingly boundless energy. It might sound like we introverts are always getting the short end of the stick, but the truth is we just process things differently. As you may remember from the previous chapter, extroverts are more focused on external rewards. As personality psychologist and fellow introvert Scott Barry Kaufman writes in an article for *Scientific American*, researchers suggest that "extraversion represents a high-intensity strategy for gaining social attention."[25] Kaufman goes on to note that the costs to being an extrovert and pursuing these rewards can result in less time and energy "that could be invested in other activities, such as accomplishing a goal (conscientiousness) or engaging with ideas and imagination (intellect/imagination)." For example, an extrovert friend of mine didn't complete her master's degree because she was so busy talking to people in the campus library that she couldn't actually sit down to finish her thesis!

Every strength can be a weakness, and every weakness can be a strength. It depends on the situation. And when it comes to introversion and extroversion, one is not better than the other; they are just different ways of being.

One of my favorite examples of this rule doesn't involve introversion. Instead, it involves another group of people whose strengths are not appreciated in American culture. Temple Grandin is a professor of animal science at Colorado State University. In her 2010 TED talk, "The World Needs All Kinds of Minds," she described how her intense focus on details, a product of her autism, enables her to understand the psychology and behavior of animals in ways few neurotypical people can. Grandin's strengths enabled her to design animal enclosures that led to less suffering and distress in the animals. Today, half the cattle in the United States are handled in facilities that she has designed.[26] (I want to note here that I have been asked by several extroverts whether introversion lies on the autism spectrum. That is a misconception; they are two separate concepts. However, the labels *introvert* and *autistic* do share a common theme—people who are not like them may refuse to accept them as they are and may discount their strengths.)

Many workplace activities, like speaking up in meetings, can be both an opportunity to showcase our strengths and a situation that reveals our weaknesses. The key is to embrace your strengths and to maneuver yourself in the right way to show off your strengths. For example, many amazing introvert public speakers excel because they are so comfortable with rehearsing, instead of winging, their speeches. If you can't shape your entire job to primarily use your strengths, as Temple Grandin did with aspects of autism, try looking at specific tasks on your to-do list and seeing if there are any opportunities to let your introvert strengths shine through, or volunteer to work on projects that use these strengths, particularly if they use your square-peg advantage—a combination of strengths that you have and that most of your coworkers do not.

Rewriting Weaknesses as Strengths

In resumes and performance reviews, or just in our own language when we're talking to ourselves, it can be helpful to rephrase our weaknesses as strengths. I'm not trying to sugarcoat all of our weaknesses here, or wallpaper over our flaws. Instead, I want to shift our focus to what's really present in our actions without the toxic concepts of who we "should" be. *See table on page 44.*

Overthinking, and Overthinking, and Overthinking

Speaking of strengths sometimes being weaknesses, our introverted strength of deep thinking can sometimes result in over-thinking and indecisiveness.

Extroverts can be indecisive, too, of course, but their indecisiveness often looks different than ours. To avoid failing, extroverts may talk to other people and get various opinions before deciding on the next step. Meanwhile, introverts stay inside their own heads and try to think and rethink the problem, often hoping they will find a breakthrough with the power of one person's thoughts—their own. We also fear different things—extroverts may fear they will regret the result of a wrong action, while introverts may fear they will waste their time on the wrong course of action. I believe this is tied to phenomenon we previously discussed where extroverts are more sensitive to seeking rewards.

Strengths	Weaknesses
Self-starter	Prefers not to work in teams
Focuses on the task at hand	Doesn't chat as often as extroverted coworkers
Listens and then synthesizes various information into a coherent whole	May not talk in meetings as often as extroverts
An interest in going deeper into conversations	Disinterest in small talk
Can listen deeply in customer service or sales calls	Not as talkative as extroverted coworkers
Deep network	Small network
Considers things deeply and often from many angles	Dislikes being put on the spot
Needs a low-stimulation environment to recharge	Needs a low-stimulation environment to recharge

This fear of making the wrong decision can prevent both introverts and extroverts from making any decision at all. Most of the time, people look for the "best" course of action, but "best" is only something that can be gleaned from a time machine since we can rarely test every single option and see it to its completion before making a decision. In reality, all you can do is create a theory about what will be the best next step for you.

Overthinking often stems from perfectionism, which can stem from the fear of judgment. Almost nobody likes to "fail," especially publicly. But what most people forget is that if something goes wrong, it's really only considered a failure if you're not able to learn from your mistake. And oftentimes, it isn't until we fail that we can truly learn what works for us.

Action = Learning Opportunity

Let's say you hate the taste of apples and oranges. You can make a deduction and guess that you'll hate the way all fruits taste, but you won't actually know if you'll hate bananas until you try one. Repeatedly wondering if you hate bananas isn't going to tell you as much as actually trying one. Even if you confirm your hypothesis that bananas are disgusting, the act of having eaten the banana means you will no longer have to waste your resources guessing if you like them or wondering if you should try them.

To take a less silly example, it's very common for people to be indecisive about accepting a job in a new field. It feels like the stakes are high. While there are certain things you can do, like arrange informational interviews or volunteer work that can inform your decision, ultimately you still have to make a decision, and you won't have a complete understanding of what it's like to work in that field and for a certain company until you actually start the job.

It's a good skill to think before we act, but there is a point when it goes too far. Most likely, you'll even realize what's happening the moment you step into overthinking. You might even say to yourself, "I'm overthinking this." Listen to yourself when you hear those words! So often, we'll disregard our intuition and continue to fear making a decision. At this moment, we'll enter the "spiral of indecision." When we're in this spiral, we keep thinking through a decision, hoping to gain a new piece of information that will make the pathway forward clear. But oftentimes, that new piece of information will never arrive.

Because I'm an INFJ, one of the sixteen personality types based on the Myers-Briggs Type Indicator (MBTI), I base a lot of my decisions on intuition. So, if I can't make a decision after some time, I'll sometimes flip a coin: Heads = Yes, Tails = No. If it's a *yes*, but if my gut tells me I'm disappointed, then I do the opposite of the coin flip result. Likewise, if it's a *no*, and I'm disappointed by the coin flip outcome, then I do the opposite. If you don't like making decisions based on intuition, just flip the coin and follow its lead (or not).

Once you make the decision, I suggest letting go and leaving the decision-making process behind. It's time for serendipity to take over.

Thriving Introvert Corner with Fiona—You Are Your Own Best Advocate

Fiona is a good friend of mine who was able to secure her own private office at her work—*and* she works from home two days a week. Pretty much every introvert's dream. I wanted to interview her and find out which introvert strengths she used to secure the office and remote working days. Turns out, she used her skills in preparation, looking at the big picture, and plenty of hard work and diligence.

> **Thea:** How were you able to convince your boss to let you work from home two days a week?

> **Fiona:** I used to work in a cubicle, but one of my coworkers was extremely loud and intrusive, making my transcription work much harder than it needed to be. I also had a very long commute, which was taking a toll on my health and made me miss some days at work. One day, when I couldn't make it into the office for health reasons, I worked from home, which turned out great. So, I asked my boss if I could work from home since my work is all digital. We trialed it and realized that my work quality was much better, and I did more work in the same amount of time. If you're thinking about approaching your boss, always ask for a trial and do your best from home—but don't overdo it as well. You don't want them to think you're not working hard when you're in the office.

Thea: And how were you able to get your own private office?

Fiona: Someone who had the office space retired. As soon as my boss made the announcement of his retirement, I went into his office and told him that out of everyone in the workplace, I needed the quiet the most since I was doing transcription. Someone else who had been at the company longer was expecting the office, but I made sure to ask for the office before she did. And when I did ask, I made sure I presented well-thought out reasons as to why I should get it. I was also prepared to quit if I didn't get the office.

Thea: And when you told your boss that you would quit if you didn't get the office, were you afraid he would let you quit?

Fiona: There are things I know how to do that the interns and my coworkers can't do, so I have some job security. But I know I can't—and I don't think anyone can—afford to be complacent. Even when I'm on vacation, I still do last-minute work.

Thea: How do you make sure you're doing great work at home?

Fiona: Everything's scheduled. I schedule in lunch and a fifteen-minute break. I also have a designated area to do my work in. I have one computer for my personal life and another for work. Otherwise, I would just jump onto Facebook.

Thea: Do you have any other tips for introverts who
    want to work from home?

Fiona: It's really important to have clear communica-
    tion. Once a week, I sit down with my boss and
    we go over the calendar. That way, I'll know if he
    has something that is deadline-driven and I'll be
    able to schedule in time to do last-minute work. I
    know that if I can't get all my work done at home,
    they might take the privilege away. We also keep
    in contact over texts throughout the workday.

Thea: So you have a lot of built-in trust with your boss.

Fiona: Yes.

Use Your Square-Peg Advantage to Stand Out

The key to standing out is not blending in. One way to do that is
to volunteer for projects that will allow you to use your natural
skills, skills that other members in your team may not have. This
way, you'll set yourself up for success when you work on the tasks
that fit you well and that your other team members may not want
to do.

> You're a square peg in a workplace with
> round pegs—use that advantage!

You can even use your square-peg advantage to do self-promotion. If it seems like everyone at your workplace is loudly

tooting their own horn, then, by definition, you won't stand out if you do the same. There are other opportunities for you to stand out in your own way, perhaps by creating stellar work and then—and this is key—quietly but confidently sharing your accomplishments.

Jennifer Yuh Nelson, director of the films *Kung Fu Panda 2* and *Kung Fu Panda 3*, didn't rise in the ranks of animation studios because she constantly boasted about her successes or told everyone who would or wouldn't listen how great she was. In an interview with the Center for Asian American Media, Jennifer noted, "I didn't talk my way into a job. Because I'm not that giddily social and extroverted of a person—I'm quite introverted." She went on to say, "When the producers had scripts, I said, 'Could I take one page and try it, just for me?' I would draw it, I would show them what I could do. It didn't require talking them into it. It's just showing them, this is what I could do for you. And then, they would go, 'Here's the rest of the script.' That's how I got my first storyboarding job."[27]

One of the things that's awesome about Jennifer's experience is that she tooted her own horn *her* way. She didn't shout, but she did take the initiative and ask for that one page.

As introverts, we have strengths and talents that make us valuable members of any team. Whether you grew up in an extrovert-focused or introvert-focused society, and whether you believe you are broken or have a self-confidence that is made of steel, you are part of a worldwide community of introverts who can thrive in the workplace.

"My introverted strength allowed me to study people, especially in meetings. This helped me to assess the best strategy for a project. I knew how to allocate personnel according to their strengths."

—Nancy, former director of clinical services

III.

THE CULTURE OF NORMAL

Why is it that workplace meetings aren't set up for everyone to thrive? Why are open office spaces such a huge fad when it's probably a nightmare for 56.8 percent of the world's population? By understanding nature, nurture, and how culture shapes what we consider normal and what we consider abnormal, we can start to comprehend why your boss doesn't understand, say, your dislike of workplace parties. And once we get to the root of a problem, it becomes easier to solve.

While most of this book assumes that you live in an extrovert-focused society, even if you live in an introvert-focused culture, this chapter will still help you understand why some of your friends and coworkers act differently from you and why they may pressure you to be like them.

We're Not So Different from the Olive Flounder

Ethologists, people who study animal behavior, have found that individual olive flounders, a type of fish, behave in different ways. Some olive flounders consistently investigate new objects, while others watch and wait to make sure everything is safe before investigating.[28] Ethologists use the words *shy* and *bold* to refer to the differences in how the individual animals respond to risks.

It's not just fish that exhibit distinct personalities; scientists have also noticed that the (unfortunately named) shy-bold continuum exists in many other animals, including seals and kangaroos. And it makes sense why this sort of spectrum would be present in various species. Bold animals will quickly find new sources of food, but if these new sources of "food" turn out to be a predator, the bold animals will be eaten; however, the shy animals will survive. A species as a whole has more chances of survival if it consists of both bold and shy individuals. Studies have suggested that there are genetic differences between shy and bold zebrafish[29] and between aggressive and fear-avoidant foxes.[30] It would appear that in nonhuman animals, individuals have some instincts and "ways of being" that are determined by genetics.

I Ran

It's not just fish and seals and kangaroos that have a consistent personality. Sometimes, humans engage in certain responses, such as freezing or fleeing, that are purely instinctual. Like that time I ran away from friendly cows . . .

We were walking along the route of Hadrian's Wall, an ancient wall in what is now northern England. Construction of the wall began in 122 CE by the Roman emperor Hadrian to demarcate the northern boundary of the Roman Empire in Britain. Little of the original Hadrian's Wall exists today, but the basic route along the wall is still known, and countless tourists each year take roughly seven days to walk across the width of England. Parts of the current route pass through city landscapes and others through the classic English countryside.

I hadn't realized when we started our cross-country journey that the countryside would pose a problem for me. I am not a country person; I am a city person. Large (and many small) animals scare me. I cannot predict their behavior, and therefore my default assumption is that they will chase or try to hurt me. And, indeed, some of them have—I don't think I will ever get over my fear of geese. To be clear, I like animals and would never hurt them; I don't even squash spiders. I'm just irrationally scared of most animals and expect them to attack me unprovoked.

My wife and I were about halfway through our walk and had reached one particularly lush field in the English countryside. To my right was a newly built stone wall several feet taller than me, and to my left was a countryside pasture with five cows peacefully grazing. We had been walking across the green grass for ten minutes, maybe more, and were following the route of the stone wall on our right that seemingly stretched on forever, when I noticed movement out of the corner of my eye. I looked to my left. The cows that had been grazing just moments before were now running in our direction. (My wife, when reading through this section, wrote the comment: "I remember them just ambling quickly.") Without thinking, I started sprinting away from the charging cows. I kept running. And running. I eventually reached the end of the wall and slipped around the corner to hide. I stood there for a few seconds to catch my breath and, realizing my wife hadn't yet appeared beside me, hesitantly looked around the corner of the wall. My wife was calmly walking toward me, and the cows were calmly standing in the field looking at her. Fortunately, my wife was just amused; by that time, she had known for years that we have very different thresholds for self-preservation. (I am so embarrassed and not at all proud that I had left my wife to fend for herself against the cows as I ran for my life!)

In that moment, running was not a "decision" I had consciously made; it was an instinct that kicked in when I believed I was in a life-threatening circumstance. I had experienced the automatic fight-or-flight instinct, a biological instinct of self-preservation. If I had stopped to think, I would have not only decided to stand by my wife so we could fight the cows together, but I would have also realized that those cows had less reason to kill me and more reason to walk briskly toward greener grass.

Our fight-or-flight instinct isn't the only behavior that's based in biology. As we discussed in Chapter I, we know from studies of sets of twins that introversion and extroversion are also biologically based. We do not choose our natural predisposition for introversion or extroversion. You were most likely born an introvert and are naturally predisposed to finding a quiet room relaxing, for example, just as an olive flounder is born with a predisposition to explore or to stay safe. This biologically based way of being is referred to as *temperament*.

Just a Pile of Feathers

The European red robin was seeing red, literally and figuratively. He had spotted a red robin rival and was ready to attack. If he could speak English, he would probably have said, "Hell no, this is my turf," maybe with a few expletives thrown in to intimidate the enemy that stood in front of him. Except there was no red robin standing in front of him on the forest floor; there was just a clump of red and white feathers that had been placed there by researchers.[31]

To me and you, this red robin had reacted illogically (as I had with the cows). But logical thought had nothing to do with it. The robin was simply following through with the instructions given to him by his genetic code that said "specific shade of red = attack." In order for genetic code to influence our fight-or-flight instinct, it has to allow us to draw quick assumptions based on sometimes very incomplete evidence if we find ourselves in the face of a potential life-or-death situation.

We Are Pattern Makers

We've established that introverts have powerful strengths, that we make up 56.8 percent of the global population, and that our temperament is a predisposition based on our biology. So why do some societies think we're defective? It has to do with a form of automatic decision making—an unconscious mental shortcut or assumption that I call *mental autofill.*

An autofill is when you go to the checkout page of an online store and you find your name and address are already filled in. It's different from an autocomplete, which is what happens when a search engine into which you are entering key words provides suggestions as you type. Mental autofills don't politely offer suggestions like autocompletes. With mental autofills, a story is already created in your mind about the way the world works, and how you need to respond in order to survive and thrive.

It's not just humans that have mental autofills; all animals use similar shortcuts to make sense of the world and to survive.

For instance, every creature's life depends on the ability to quickly categorize items into "safe or poison" and "safe or predator." In order to survive, all animals must be able to observe patterns and quickly categorize objects, even objects they've never seen before, and then make decisions about those objects, just like the European red robin.

Humans, of course, are constantly faced with much more complicated and nuanced decisions than "safe or poison." We don't know how many decisions a person has to make every day, but the answer is most likely in the thousands. One study theorized that we make an average of 221 decisions just regarding food each day.[32] If we had to start from scratch to make these decisions, and if each decision about food took six and a half minutes, we would have used up the entire twenty-four hours just deciding on what to eat! That explains why, most of the time, we make split-second decisions based on the unconscious patterns we've created about how the world works and how we should behave in accordance with them.

The Culture of Fruit Flies

Autofills don't just exist to help us avoid predators or ingest enough nutrition to survive. Autofills are also created by culture. Culture, "the collective programming of the mind that distinguishes the members of one group or category of people from others,"[33] exists among both humans and animals. A study published in *Science* magazine found that "fruitflies have five cognitive capacities that enable them to transmit mating preferences culturally across generations."[34] In that study, female fruit flies were able to choose between two mates, for instance, a green or pink mate. They didn't seem to care about the color of their mate, and both colors were chosen equally. However, a separate female fruit fly who had witnessed one of the original fruit flies choosing a mate went on to pick a mate of that same color. So, if a female fruit fly witnessed her peer choosing a green mate, that individual would choose a green mate, too.

Why does culture exist in animals, and why do humans have culture? Ken Binmore, in a paper called "Why did Fairness Norms Evolve?" believes that "like monkeys, we are programmed to imitate the behaviour of our more successful neighbors."[35] It seems that imitation, and the belief that those arbitrary choices are logical, is part of our genetic programming.

You and I have free will, and we can choose to imitate our successful neighbors or to go down a different path. But no matter what we choose, we are still part of a culture. As W. G. Runciman, a leading British historical sociologist, writes, "once you have decided to do what you then proceed to do, your behaviour becomes part of the large-scale collective behaviour-pattern[,] which makes the distinctive culture and society of which you are a member."[36] We are all part of a culture—and most likely a member of a subculture, as well. The culture that surrounds us determines what we consciously and subconsciously consider "normal."

Cultural Autofills

As children grow up, we cannot teach them how to react to every single circumstance they come across; instead, it's necessary for them to create guesses or snap judgments based on rules they have already learned. The ability to guess, and to be surprised when something unexpectedly goes wrong, happens at an extremely young age. In fact, it doesn't matter if an infant is learning to speak English or Cantonese; one of the first ten words they are likely to say is the equivalent of the English word *uh-oh*, meaning, "I did not expect something bad to happen."[37] In general, humans dislike ambiguity—since our survival depends on us quickly categorizing the world into black and white—so creating theories about the world, acting on those theories, and assuming these theories hold true in subsequent scenarios is a basic aspect of human behavior that starts at a very early age.

To complicate things, the number of lessons children learn to keep them physically safe from harm pales in comparison to another type of lesson they intentionally or involuntarily absorb: lessons that teach them how to blend into what other members of their society consider "the norm."

My siblings and I were taught to use a fork when eating; that was "the norm" in our culture. If we had grown up in a different culture, we might have been taught to use chopsticks instead. We were also taught not to burp at the table; but in a different culture, burping might be considered a compliment to the person who cooked the meal. In other words, we learned rules—either directly or indirectly through observation—that dictated how we should fit into our society's "normal." The lessons we learn about culture as children will continue to affect us when we grow into adults.

As adults, we don't just use mental autofills when we're faced with a rival for a mate, like our friend the red robin; or when we're deciding on what we'll eat for lunch; or when we're faced in life-or-death situations, such as when a few cows run toward us. We also use cultural autofills—shortcuts—to help us decide if certain behaviors are considered "normal," and therefore accepted and praised, in our society.

The Other Normal

It's crucial to know that the cultural autofills of our society that define what is considered the "norm" are not always correct, accurate, or helpful—especially when it comes to misconceptions about introversion. On Facebook, I once read a comment by an extrovert who shared that she had "trained" her introverted husband to make small talk with the service staff who took his order at drive-through windows because she believed it was rude for him to not ask how their day was going. I strongly disagree. I think pretending to have an interest in another person's day when you don't actually have the energy or interest for a discussion is, in fact, rude and insincere. There are many other ways to convey to a person that you sincerely see them and acknowledge them: a friendly smile, the tone of your voice, a dollar in the tip jar. Unfortunately, introverted sincerity isn't what matters in an extrovert-focused society such as the one found in my home country of the United States. Instead, we're expected to play by the cultural rules set by extroverts, even if they don't make sense to us.

This extrovert bias certainly doesn't exist in every country. In some countries, such as Finland, introversion is considered normal. Afnan, an introvert from Pakistan, a country with an extrovert bias, is currently living in Finland. He says Finnish people, "tend to keep to themselves unless they really need to talk to you. It's an act of respecting each other's personal space." Sounds amazing to this introvert!

We already know that introverts make up at least 56.8 percent of the global population, making us, by definition, normal. So why do people in the US and many other countries consider introverted traits to be a personality defect?

Me-Colored Glasses

The phrase *rose-colored glasses* is used when someone sees only the good in a certain situation and can't see its bad aspects. Well, we're all walking around with "me-colored glasses" that interpret what we see through our own set of autofills.

You may have heard of the golden rule: treat others the way *you* want to be treated. But have you heard of the platinum rule: treat others the way *they* want to be treated? The problem with the platinum rule is that while we may try our best to be empathetic, we cannot literally step into someone else's shoes. It's impossible. We can only guess, and our guesses are influenced by our "me-colored glasses."

When you combine the concept of me-colored glasses with the concept of an autofill created by a culture that has socialized you to adopt a set of learned behaviors, you can get a society that continues to hold up certain myths about introversion, such as thinking introverts can become extroverts—or should strive to become extroverts—if we would only just try hard enough. While some extroverts are very open minded, there are others who have a very strong prescription of me-colored glasses. They think that other people are governed by the same inner workings that govern them. And if they grew up in an extrovert-focused society, which confirms the "normal" of their own extroverted personality and sends the message that introverts are broken, then you'll get extroverts pushing you to attend a party because they love parties and just can't compute why you don't sincerely love them, too. You'll get a culture that says "Why are you so quiet?" much more often than "Why can't you stop talking and just enjoy the silence?" Imagine a society where it's "normal" for an introvert to pushily insist that their extroverted friend have a quiet night alone on a Friday by staying home and reading a book with a cat on their lap. That certainly doesn't exist here in the United States!

The Me-Colored Glasses that Pushed Marsha Away

Marsha was trained to use canned phrases and slimy tactics to close sales at her job. She hated feeling inauthentic, so she developed her own style of actively listening to customers in order to assess their needs, versus throwing a sales pitch at them. Her approach to sales worked for her, and she became a top-performing sales person, consistently reaching 200 percent above her sales goals.

Unfortunately, the prescription on her boss's me-colored glasses were so strong that Marsha wasn't congratulated on her successes. Instead, her personality was constantly belittled. Marsha's boss often made comments like: "I have no idea how someone so quiet could be making all these sales." Marsha eventually left the firm, and the company lost a good employee because their me-colored glasses were kept firmly on.

Tips for Managing Introverts

Many introverts (and extroverts) find that recognition at work is important to their happiness. Have a conversation with your report about how they prefer to be recognized. Some people love bonuses, and some would actually rather receive a sincere compliment than a few extra dollars. Most introverts will prefer praise to be given one-to-one, but perhaps your introverted report would like to be acknowledged publicly with an award.

Don't make an assumption based on your own preferences, or based on preferences you see in other introverted reports. Instead, ask each individual what they prefer.

Rewriting the Autofill

When you are confronted with an autofill in the workplace that undermines your strengths, here's what you can do:

1. Rewrite it
2. Go with it
3. Leave it

1. Rewrite it.

When I moved to the United Kingdom from America, I had to rewrite a very ingrained autofill—which side of the road cars drive down. It took over two years to rewrite that concept of normal, but eventually it became instinctual to first look to the right (instead of first looking to the left) before crossing the street. If I can rewrite an everyday activity such as crossing the street, you can also work to rewrite a longstanding cultural autofill. For instance, your boss may have inaccurate autofills and misconceptions related to introversion and leadership. With time and the opportunity to exhibit your leadership skills on important projects—and if your boss is a good manager—you can rewrite this autofill. Prove that you can bust their myth by being a good introvert leader.

But what about if you don't have a good boss?

2. Go with it.

Despite your best efforts, autofills may be difficult to rewrite, and sometimes, it just makes sense to go with the flow, depending on the situation. I'm a believer in picking and choosing which autofills to fight. This is particularly important for introverts who get drained by conflict.

You can also use the situation to your advantage. It might work out in your favor if your boss would rather put the office extrovert on customer service duties, especially if you don't like speaking to clients (though remember that introverts can make great customer service representatives, too—for example, because of our natural listening skills). Essentially, take on projects that will allow you to highlight your unique introvert strengths so you can still be seen as a valuable team member.

3. Leave it.

If you have a terrible boss, like Marsha did, and their autofills are negatively affecting your mental health, start updating your resume! You can at least consider moving to a new team at the same company, or even leaving the company entirely and working somewhere else.

You Are Not Broken

If your culture has a heavy bias toward extroversion and refuses to acknowledge your strengths (and is therefore missing out on the wealth of your talents), it is the society that is broken, not you.

Even if you have internalized an autofill that says you can't find success because of your temperament, I can pretty much guarantee you that there is an introvert out there somewhere who has proven that assumption wrong. Introverts can't be leaders? What about Mary Barra, CEO of General Motors?[38] Introverts are too timid to direct movies? Jennifer Yuh Nelson has directed several films, including the very popular *Kung Fu Panda 2*. Introverts aren't promoted? What about Julie Zhuo, who started working at Facebook as a software engineer intern in 2006 and is now their vice president of design?

To thrive in the workplace, we need to carry off a balancing act: we need to honor the innate strengths of our introversion, while being constantly aware that our colleagues and bosses may be interpreting our external actions in potentially inaccurate ways. In the next chapter, I'll provide you with the tools to help widen your beam.

"By distilling the information gleaned from various sources during project meetings, I'm able to put forward a workable plan rather than simply asking, 'How's that going to work?'"

—Julia, former IT project manager

IV.

YOUR "THRIVING INTROVERT" TOOLBOX

Introverts are not failed extroverts. Introverts are not broken. No matter what cultural autofills may say, we are whole human beings who have innate strengths that we carry around with us everywhere. And our strengths are powerful.

In a way, extroverts are like fireworks, while introverts are like candles. In certain situations, the softest introverts will illuminate the room, while in other situations the loudest extroverts can blind. You already have a wealth of tools in your introvert toolbox, and you'll need to get familiar with the specific tools necessary for thriving in an extrovert-focused workplace.

In this chapter, I'll share a lifetime's worth of tips and tricks I've learned about navigating the workplace, as well as everyday life as an introvert. Some of these concepts I use myself, while others I've developed for introvert clients with personalities a little different to mine. We'll lay the foundation for tapping into your hidden talents and learn how to capitalize on your natural way of being while at work. I'll also show you when and how you can act in more "extroverted" ways—if the situation demands it—to achieve your career goals. We'll also go over additional tools you can add to your toolbox, such as my SPARK Method for thriving.

Let's explore the tools that can help you stay in integrity as you learn to navigate an extrovert-focused workplace.

What You Focus on Grows

Lewis Carroll's book *Alice in Wonderland* has this wonderful exchange between Alice and the Cheshire Cat:

> "Would you tell me, please, which way I ought to go
>   from here?"
> "That depends a good deal on where you want to get to,"
>   said the Cat.
> "I don't much care where—" said Alice.
> "Then it doesn't matter which way you go," said the Cat.
> "—so long as I get *somewhere*," Alice added as an
>   explanation.
> "Oh, you're sure to do that," said the Cat, "if you only
>   walk long enough."[39]

Like Alice, we can meander until we reach somewhere. Or, we can discover where it is we want to go, and walk purposefully in that direction. In particular situations, if you need to spend your energy "extroverting" in the workplace, it will help to have a destination in mind and a reason why you're stepping out of your comfort zone. We'll talk more about the concept of "extroverting" later on in this chapter.

Some introverts are unhappy that we tend to walk, rather than run, toward a destination, and some of us are jealous that extroverts have seemingly boundless energy for socializing and getting things done. I think this jealousy stems from a few misunderstandings. First, extroverts do not have boundless energy. Extroverts also need rest, and I've heard from many of them that they, too, need time alone—just not as much as introverts do. Second, expending more "extroverting" energy doesn't necessarily lead to a flourishing in life or at work. Which would you rather do—walk steadily toward your goals until you hit them, or run frantically in any direction only to find yourself miles away from happiness? The speed of getting to a random goal isn't as important as carefully choosing an authentic goal from the beginning.

The first step toward a fulfilling career and life is finding out what success and thriving mean to *you*. However, many of my new clients come to me burnt out and discouraged because they are trying to reach a version of success as defined by other people. To take a concept from Chapter III, it's possible that they have an inauthentic autofill related to what it means to thrive and what it takes to be successful. Maybe you were taught that you should move as far up the corporate ladder as possible—but once you're halfway there, you realize that pursuit feels empty. Or perhaps you were taught as a child that money and ambition is evil, and you've had to learn that it's okay to want a pay raise.

Typically, introverts are intrinsically, rather than extrinsically, motivated. Usually, what drives our behavior is our thoughts and feelings (for instance, our desire to feel confident or appreciated or creative) versus external rewards, like an employee-of-the-month award. To prevent yourself from needlessly draining your energy at work to achieve a dream you never cared about in the first place, we need to discover your personal concepts of success and thriving.

One of the most important tools in your toolbox is your intrinsic motivation, the reason you want to do well in the workplace. Your intrinsic motivation creates what I call your *why*, the reason why you are reaching for success. Alice may have been lost, but you don't need to be. Let's find your *somewhere*.

What Does Thriving Mean to You?

Introspection and looking inward for answers, not outward, is a strength of ours. Here are two classic exercises that will help you look inward and discover your why, what's truly important to you, so you can discover your authentic workplace goals.

Running into a friend

It's ten years from now, and you're at an airport. You run into a dear old friend you had lost touch with. The friend asks, "How are you doing?" And you realize you're the happiest you've ever been.

Grab a piece of paper, and for at least ten minutes, write down how you would describe to your friend the beautiful life you've created (also, assume that this friend is doing great, too, so there's no need to worry about making them feel jealous). While you should focus on describing your career in this perfect future, you can also include details about your personal life if it helps to make this exercise feel real.

Since the object of this exercise is to gain insights into what makes you uniquely happy, avoid answers that are purely luck-based, such as, "I just won the lottery and don't have to work anymore!" If you truly don't want to work anymore, write about what led up to you securing that early retirement.

There are no right or wrong answers in this exercise.

The perfect workday

In a few years, you'll have the perfect workday. Grab another piece of paper, and for at least fifteen minutes, write down what that perfect workday looks like.

If nothing is coming to mind, try to picture yourself waking up on that day, then write down what you would do next (I'm guessing you would probably not check your work email!), and what you would do after that. You can write this in essay form or as a daily itinerary. For example: "8 a.m.—wake up; 8:30 a.m.—meditate; 9:30 a.m.—make waffles and watch cartoons; 10:30 a.m.—greet the receptionist as I take the private VIP elevator to my corner office," etc.

There are no wrong answers.

Discovering the overlap

Grab another piece of paper. This time we'll be looking at the two exercises above and making note of the patterns we see that point to your idea of a happier life. First, you'll be looking for patterns in what *success* means to you, and second, you'll be looking for patterns in what *thriving* means to you. Finally, you'll be looking for patterns in what you value. Together, these three concepts will give you valuable clues about what to change in your life, work environment, or career.

1. Success patterns. Thriving and success are two different concepts. Reaching success refers to prospering externally, usually

in obtaining an object or lifestyle you desire, while thriving refers to prospering internally. Look through what you wrote in your "Running into a friend" and "The perfect workday" exercises. Did you write anything down that pertains to success and obtaining something external? Perhaps you wrote that you would be living in a different location or that you would be working from home. Perhaps you wrote that you would be making a certain amount of money or have a certain house or car. Record your ideas of success on a new sheet of paper and label it "Success Guide."

2. Thriving patterns. Look through the exercises again, but this time search for hints on what thriving—prospering internally— means to you. Perhaps you'll notice that you frequently used the words *enjoyment* and *spontaneous*. Perhaps you wrote that in the future you would feel more connected to the people around you. Label this section "Thriving Guide" and note any similarities—big or small—in how described your future inner self.

3. Value patterns. Next, look for patterns related to what you value in the work you do, as well as in the activities outside of work that you enjoy. If you notice that you mentioned participating in hobbies like painting and crafting, that could mean you value expressing your creativity or working with your hands. If you mentioned owning items like fancy watches and cars, that could mean you value having material wealth or status. Record the patterns you see under the section "Values Guide."

4. Look through your value patterns, thriving patterns, and success patterns. Most of what you noted should be inspirational. However, you might notice that some of the concepts you've written down give you a sense of unease or a sense of "heaviness," as if your mind is weighed down by those ideas. Or perhaps some of the concepts give you a knot in your stomach and make you feel a little gross. It's possible the items that give you a sense of discomfort are related to "autofills" that you've learned from your childhood, autofills that are no longer true or useful to you. For instance, maybe you've written down that you'd like to have a sports car ten years from now. However, the idea alone fills you with a heaviness, and upon reflection, you remember that your family brought you up to dislike anything that displayed material wealth. That's a sign that your values and autofills are now incongruent, and you should embrace your value and let go of that heaviness. Or it might be the opposite: you've written down that you love routine, because your current boss has drilled the idea into your head, or because you've been told it's a necessity at your current job. But the idea of routines actually fills you with a sense of unease because, deep down, you hate it when everything stays the same, day in and day out.

After some introspection, cross off the items that don't match what you actually want. Often, these crossed-out items are related to "shoulds," where you tell yourself: "I *should* want structure, because that's what everyone else wants." Sometimes inauthentic patterns can also be found in logic—for instance, you may have subconsciously told yourself: "I've already spent four years of my life getting this degree, and it's only logical that I not waste it." But when you actually think about spending the next ten years in accounting, your skin crawls. Author Seth Godin refers to the decisions we made in the past as *sunk costs*, a business term that refers to money that was spent and that can no longer be recovered. Just because you put time or effort or money into something doesn't mean it needs to still affect your decisions. I agree with Seth that sunk costs are "gifts from the you of yesterday, and it's okay to refuse them."[40] It's okay to cross off past gifts from yourself.

It's also okay to cross nothing off the list, or almost everything. What's most important is that you get a sense of what you authentically want your career and life to be like. You have the power to shape your life in big ways or small.

The one little step

It's common to look at what you've written in the "Running into a friend" and "The perfect workday" exercises and panic because that life seems unattainable and dependent on things not wholly under your control, such as promotions. But most people don't realize just how much control we have over our lives. I've found that in the quest to shine with integrity, big results can come from little changes. You can start making little changes, right now, that will bring you closer to that career and life you wrote about. Let me show you how.

Look at your success, thriving, and values patterns and pick one thing on that list that could bring you happiness. It's okay if it's not related to work. What's one little step you can take right now to bring more of that into your life? I have a very creative name for this one little step: "The one little step."

When my client Ellen did these exercises, one of the patterns she noticed was that she wanted to live in a house by the Pacific Ocean. She wanted to spend each morning eating breakfast while looking at the waves. What would you suggest her one little step be? She had already started saving up to buy a house, but even if that wasn't the case, saving up for a house takes years. We decided she didn't have to wait years before she could bring a taste of that dream into her life right now—her one little step was simply to spend more time at a coffee shop by the beach instead of in the land-locked coffee shop she usually goes to. The coffee shop by the beach was farther from her house, but it brought a little more joy into her life.

Maybe one of your dreams is to have a corner office so you can have privacy and be able to look out the window and connect with nature. You might not be able to get that corner office tomorrow, but you can still take small steps to bring it into your life now: ask your manager to let you move your desk so it faces a window, or bring in a potted plant or even a fake plant to decorate your desk.

Small steps can lead to big changes.

Don't stop at this single "one little step." I suggest turning it into a routine and scheduling fifteen minutes into your calendar each week for this activity. During that time, do some introspection and decide on your next one little step, a small action or task that will help you live a life and career built around your personality and preferences. After you've come up with your weekly small step, take it. If the step can't be done immediately, schedule it into your calendar to implement later that week.

Discovering the Overlap

For you to truly achieve your goals in the workplace, there must be some overlap between your vision of thriving and the company's vision of thriving.

Look through the exercise you've just completed to see if any of your values fit your company culture and work requirements. If you find overlapping values, plan to incorporate more of those into your job. If you discover that there is very little overlap somewhere—for example, if you value creativity but currently work in a role at a company that requires its employees to stifle their creativity, such as a cashier at a fast food chain—you might want to dig deeper or reconsider your options. Perhaps you can find more overlap in one of your other values—for example, making customers feel safe and listened to if one of your other values is kindness. Try to create more opportunities at your work to use values that are important to you.

Keep in mind that your job doesn't have to fulfill *all* of your needs. It's possible to still be happy and thrive at a job if you focus on where there is an overlap or how you can make your values matter. Some people do prefer to keep their work and passion projects separate, and you can also find an outlet for your values outside of work. If you can't express your creativity as a cashier at a fast food chain, spend your workdays focusing on your value of serving your customers well, and on the weekends, join a poetry group or write a screenplay to exercise your imagination.

If you're still not sure if your current workplace is right for you, there are a myriad of other items to look at to determine if you can flourish at your work. For instance, look at the following areas in your company to see if there is overlap:

- **Hierarchy.** How is the business structured? How do people feel or react to the structure and hierarchies present? Does the CEO ever interact with employees in lower levels? How is private office space allocated? Where do you fit in?
- **Structure.** Is it a new organization or a small organization that's receptive to input and where you may need to react to changes quickly, or is it an established business with narrow roles and clear goals?
- **Rewarded behavior.** What kind of employee behavior is rewarded? Is there a difference between how they say they reward results and what they actually do? Do you feel rewarded for good work?
- **Communication.** How open is the environment? How often do managers meet with reports? Do managers welcome feedback? Are you able to communicate your needs?
- **Company's mission and social media presence.** A company's mission, at the very least, should reveal how they want the outside world to perceive or think of them. A company's social media presence is the day-to-day manifestation of how the company wants to be seen by the public. Do you see overlap in the way they are presenting themselves to the outside world and your values?
- **Customer service model.** A customer service model tells you how the company treats their clients. Does it resonate with the way you operate? Zappos, a large online retailer (whose CEO, Tony Hsieh, is an

introvert), states on its website: "Our purpose is simple: to live and deliver WOW." The website also boasts that its longest customer service call is 10 hours and 43 minutes—after helping a customer with an order, the Zappos employee and customer started chatting and kept talking for hours![41] Based on this, Zappos may not be the best company for someone unwilling to go above and beyond or for those uninterested in connecting with customers; on the flip side, introverts looking to make meaningful connections with the people they serve might find value in this.

Once you discover how the company you work for operates, you'll be able to see if there's enough overlap in values and visions to support your growth and happiness while you're there. If there isn't currently much of an overlap and you can't see how to create one, are you willing to stay in the job and pursue your values outside of work?

Make Your Boss Look Good

Of course, it's not just an overlap of values that will determine if you can thrive at your job. The people you work with also affect your happiness at work, as well as your ability to do your work. One of the most important people at your job will be your immediate supervisor, and that person may have a different set of values than you. Your supervisor will also have their own idea of what your "thriving" should look like, and they will look to you for help in reaching *their* own work goals.

Many years ago, I saw a YouTube video by Guy Kawasaki, an early Apple employee and an introvert, who shared the most important advice I've heard regarding success in the workplace: *Make your boss look good.* In an article on rocking your first ninety days of a job, Kawasaki expanded on this concept: "If you make your boss look good, your career path will be better, faster, and easier because a rising tide floats all boats."[42] I believe this piece of advice has two meanings. First, if you want your boss's job, it needs to be vacant. If your boss gets a promotion, even if it's solely because of your hard work, guess what job is available? There's also a second way to look at this advice. If you're just starting out in the working world, it's easy to think that the way to succeed is simply to "be the best at your job." That's how you got As in school, right? If you're a little more experienced, you probably know by now that it's not enough just to focus on your own work; there are a myriad of other expectations and other people's values that you have to meet in the workplace—most important of which are your boss's expectations of your work, even if it doesn't match what you think your best work should look like. You need to spend your energy not just satisfying your goals, but your boss's goals as well.

Guy Kawasaki has another perspective-changing piece of advice: if your supervisor asks you to do something, do it, and do it quickly. Even if you think there are other more important tasks to be finished first, or even if you think that it's a nonsensical request, that task is at the forefront of her mind. She is clearly telling you her priorities. It may be the case that *her* boss just asked her to get it done, or that she has access to facts that you may not know, such as there being an inspection coming through. The point is, you may not have the full context to make the right judgment call. Once you've completed the task, don't forget to let your boss know—you are now "the worker who gets things done," and she'll know she can always count on you.

I know someone who followed this advice. Her supervisor required every staff member to fill out a statistics form every month. This employee didn't think it was a very good representation of the work they were doing, and the staff all thought it was a waste of time, but the supervisor received each form personally and would send reminders if the forms were late. This employee made sure to have her form filled out and sent to her boss by the start of the business day on the first of every month. When the time for annual reviews came around, the first evidence her supervisor brought up was regarding how organized and dedicated she was was the timely statistics forms, even though she was hardworking and good at her job in many other aspects.

Whether you're always on the same page as your supervisor, or the two of you don't see things eye-to-eye, remember to keep their values in mind.

The SPARK Method

Once you understand your values, and the values of your manager, the next step is: actually thriving! How do you start?

I came up with the SPARK Method for my clients who were stressed and facing autofills and a lack of confidence at work. Even if you're confident at work, you can still use the SPARK Method at any point in your career and with (pretty much) any problem, including ones that require stepping out of your comfort or effortless zone. If you find that you get the most out of just one the following five concepts, but don't find the others to be very useful, that's totally fine. You'll always have these concepts at your disposal if you need them.

S - SUPPORT

P - PREPARE

A - ACHIEVEMENT

R - RELEASE

K - KICKASS

S - Support: You might prefer to gather an in-person posse of people who will be present whenever you need help at the drop of a hat, or you might prefer to seek support by joining a close-knit online community. Whatever kind of support you choose, know that you also have a hidden source of hundreds of thousands of supporters—whether it's from the books at a library or through online resources and groups. There's always someone else out there who has good and relevant advice for you no matter what you're trying to achieve, even if it's a particularly challenging problem.

P - Prepare: The art of preparation is one of the many innate superpowers that most introverts have. It really is! Our tendency to want to prepare instead of jumping in headfirst (particularly if you're an HSP, a Highly Sensitive Person) is a skill that can be used at any point in our career. This superpower has helped me to land jobs and make great presentations at meetings because I prepared first. Let's embrace our tendency to prepare instead of fighting it.

A - Achievement: "If you see it, you can be it." It may be a cheesy quote, but it's true. It's much easier to achieve something challenging once we see that other people have been able to do it.

It's also much easier to achieve something once we remember our past achievements, even if the circumstances are a little different. Maybe you've never made a presentation in front of a CEO before, but you may have gotten an A on a class presentation when you were ten. Our past achievements, no matter how small they seem or how long ago they occurred, can count for something when we need a boost in our self-esteem.

R - Release: Have you ever wanted to ace something so bad that you turned into a giant ball of stress and anxiety because of the internal pressure to succeed? Life is stressful enough! You don't need that extra stress, especially if you're an anxious HSP who may already find much of life to be overwhelming. Release that anxiety out into the wild, to be free. One way to do this is through meditation, which we'll discuss later in this chapter.

K - Kickass: When we're faced with a problem that prevents us from thriving or being our best selves, at the end of the day, it helps to remember that we're already kickass individuals. We're action-takers. We're resilient. I'm a believer in inhabiting your natural confidence, and we all have a natural confidence; it's what motivated you to take your first step (literally or metaphorically) toward independent mobility. You have confidence built in you! I'm not talking about the kind of confidence that believes you're the best thing ever; I'm talking about a confidence in your own resourcefulness, the confidence that you will, eventually, achieve what you set out to do despite the challenges. You are resilient!

> You already have the spark to thrive!

So, if you ever find yourself stressed out, pick up one of the SPARK Method tools in your toolbox and remember that there is always someone out there who will support you, that preparing is a superpower, that whatever you are facing now you have faced before, and that you were born already sparking and resilient!

Why Have a Mentor?

Most introverts are very independent. We want to figure things out ourselves. So whenever we need to get an outside opinion, we often just turn to a Google search. While the hive mind of the internet contains an amazing wealth of information, it's not always the best place to go for specific help. What a mentor can do that the internet can't is tailor their advice to you and your exact circumstance. Plus, the advice you get from the internet might be from an extrovert, so what you read could lead to more frustration. Time and time again, I see introverts thinking that they are broken and can't reach their goals because cookie-cutter advice from the internet, like "just get over it and network," simply doesn't work for them. Instead, reach out to someone you admire for help.

Since we introverts are often hyper-focused on our energy needs, you may feel weird about the idea of imposing on someone else's social energy to ask for guidance. You may also feel like asking for help is the same as being needy, a sign of weakness. But consider that this point of view may be an autofill that's no longer serving you.

Instead, try to step inside the shoes of someone who has hard-earned experience, perhaps even decades of knowledge about a certain subject. Instead of feeling bothered by someone who is asking for advice, they may in fact be flattered. They might also feel like they're giving back and investing in their legacy by helping you.

In the book *The Making of a Manager: What to Do When Everyone Looks to You*, fellow introvert Julie Zhuo points out that approaching someone with the question "Will you be my mentor?" will likely sound needy, and their answer may not be what you had hoped for. Instead, ask for specific advice, and you'll find plenty of people willing to share their experience and expertise. A mentorship doesn't necessarily have to be formal.[43]

There are plenty of people—introverts and extroverts—who would love to share their knowledge and expertise with you, if you ask for help.

Thriving Introvert Corner with Beth Cubbage— Succeeding through Mentorship

How can introverts benefit from mentorship? I turned to Beth Cubbage—a consulting manager at a software company, and owner of the business Parent Lightly, "the working mom's guide to everything"—to find out more about her experience with having a mentor.

> **Thea:** I think some introverts may feel weird about asking for guidance or be afraid of imposing on someone else's social energy. Was that something you struggled with?
>
> **Beth:** I think that's why growing an existing relationship into an organic mentorship worked so well for me. My mentorships were forged from having already worked with someone on difficult projects, so I

knew I could ask them for advice any time. On the other hand, I *have* felt guilty about imposing on mentors who have simply been assigned to me, and I haven't truly engaged.

Thea: Could you expand on what you mean by mentorships that were forged through "difficult projects"? Were you looking for a mentor at that time, and how did that mentorship play out?

Beth: I manage a team of consultants. Right after I was promoted to that role, my team and I took on a project with a challenging customer. We had to negotiate (and renegotiate) contracts, project milestones, and deliverables. The customer was really challenging. I worked with two women who were senior to me, and they both taught me so much about managing clients and people. We really bonded going through that tough yearlong project together, and I still go to both women for career advice five-plus years later.

Thea: What was the most valuable thing you received from that mentorship?

Beth: The mentorship helped me learn some tough but necessary lessons about leadership. Early in my career, I didn't get much constructive criticism. I am so grateful that these mentors trusted me enough to tell me whenever I was screwing something up. It wasn't pleasant to hear, but that advice helped me develop into the leader I am today.

Thea: What advice would you give a fellow introvert
who thinks they can benefit from a mentor?

Beth: I would say to look among the people you already
know! I think we have this idea that a mentor has to
be a big deal, like an Obi-Wan Kenobi or something.
No! A mentor is anyone who has any experience
you lack and who is willing to give you honest feedback and guidance. I also think that comfort level
is key. Introverts are great at opening up and going
deep if we are comfortable with someone. We are
much less likely to go there with someone we don't
know. I also personally feel awkward if I'm going
into a relationship trying to turn it into a mentoring
relationship. I would say that introverts shouldn't
force it. Just be open and make genuine connections with people whose work you admire.

Our Negative Autofills with Being Heard and Noticed

One of the most common issues introverts face is that it's hard
for them to self-promote and be heard. We introverts have countless autofills (assumptions our brains make regarding the way
the world works) that can make being heard or noticed particularly tough for us. As we've discussed, sometimes these autofills
are learned from culture. A past Australian client of mine grew
up hearing the phrase "Tall poppies get cut"—that is, the people
who stand out from the crowd are asking to be attacked and cut
down. The phrase had a lasting effect on how she showed up in

the world. It's not just Australia; in Nordic countries, this is called the Law of Jante; and there's also that English proverb (which you probably haven't heard if you're in the United States): "A big tree attracts the woodsman's axe."[44]

The Tall Poppy concept is so old that it's been traced to the ancient Greek historian Herodotus, who, in the fifth century BCE, wrote a story about Periander, the king of Corinth, a city state in Greece. Herodotus writes that Periander sent a messenger to visit tyrant leader Thrasybulus in order to ask for advice on how to best govern a city. Thrasybulus led the messenger to a field, where he proceeded to cut off the tallest ears of wheat. When the messenger relayed what happened, Periander believed that "Thrasybulus had counselled him to slay those of his townsmen who were outstanding in influence or ability" and followed through with that advice.[45] Tall Poppy Syndrome may have very old roots, though luckily for us today, we know that autofills can be rewritten.

Our heard and noticed autofills can also be biological in nature. For an HSP introvert, the desire to not be noticed may be influenced by the need for physical safety, and not standing out in a crowd may come down to retaining a sense of control. Standing out means that we are drawing attention to ourselves, and we won't have control over whether that attention will turn out to be positive or negative. You can't stop being an HSP, but you can start to rewrite the autofills about your relationship to the world and whether the attention is worth it.

For introverts at the other end of the spectrum, you may have no problem with speaking your mind; however, your past bluntness—which you probably call being efficient and cutting out unnecessary small talk—may have resulted in the lack of in-house advocates or workplace friends, making you reluctant to speak out in the future. Again, you can rewrite this autofill that bluntness always leads to pain; instead, search for advocates and allies, in-house or online, who appreciate this trait of yours.

You may have autofills that you picked up from culture or that are influenced by biology. But the good news is these autofills, no matter how real they seem, can be rewritten into something closer to your authentic truth!

Steps to Being Heard and Noticed

We've previously discussed that because of preconceived introvert stereotypes—that we're all shy and unassuming, for example—many people presume all managers and executives have extroverted personality traits. But that's far from the case. The world is filled with examples of introverted CEOs and business owners, from Tony Hsieh, CEO of the online shoe and clothing store Zappos, to Douglas Conant, former CEO of the Campbell Soup Company, to Melanie Perkins, CEO of Canva, a popular online graphic-design tool. Not only can introverts get promoted (and we are promoted often), but we also can be promoted to the highest office in the company! (If that's one of our goals.) And we also have the leadership skills necessary to create a successful business from the ground up.

Sadly, one of the most common problems I've seen with my fellow introverts is that we feel uncomfortable with self-promotion, which in turn can affect whether or not we are promoted in the workplace.

Fortunately, with a few simple tweaks, you can start feeling more at ease with self-promotion and advocating for yourself at work:

1. Reframe. Change your definition of self-promotion from "make myself noticed at work" to "highlight my skills and accomplishments at work." This simple act of reframing moves your focus away from *you*, as a person, and instead toward *your work*. When you start believing in this reframe, self-promotion stops feeling gross and like you're full of yourself, and starts feeling like you're helping to move the company forward by highlighting a job that has been done well—it just happens that it was *you* who did that job well.

The way you go about creating this reframe depends on your personality. If you love mantras, you may want to repeat to yourself each morning the words "Today, I will be helping the company by highlighting my skills and accomplishments at work." If you dislike that method, get a friend who can serve as an accountability partner and who will check in with you weekly about what you've done to "highlight your skills and accomplishments at work." What other things can you do to make this reframe "stick"?

2. Connect with your *why*. What positive things can being seen and heard do for your life and career? This is not the time for wondering if you're worthy of being seen and heard or for worrying about the downsides to a promotion or raise. You can think about that later. For now, think about your *why* behind wanting to be seen and heard. This may be the same *why* that you discovered earlier in this chapter with the "Running into a friend" and "The perfect workday" exercises.

When you have a good reason for expanding your comfort zone, a reason that you're passionate about, promoting yourself will become so much easier. You won't be "highlighting your skills and accomplishments at work" just for the sake of it; you'll be doing it for reasons x, y, and z. For some people, their biggest reason is their children; for others, it may be to buy a house; and for others, it may be to make a difference in the world. Or, you may really just want a Lamborghini. Whatever the reason, focus on that *why*.

3. Get clear on your accomplishments. Don't sell yourself short. The company you work for wants to retain talent, so selling yourself short won't help you or them. Update your resume, and take a good look at what you've accomplished. Once you've reminded yourself of all you've accomplished so far (don't forget to include facts and figures if you have access to them), and rehearsed talking about your achievements, you'll be ready if and when these topics come up in a meeting. And if you start tracking your accomplishments and make note of positive feedback going forward, you'll also be all set for your annual review!

4. Don't diminish your accomplishments in public. You may be tempted to attribute the success of a project to the whole team, when in reality you did 95 percent of the work. Of course, credit the other contributors to the project, but do not diminish your role in its success. Your employers want to replicate that success and retain talent, and the more accurate the information you give them, the better off you and the company will be.

5. Gather support. Through one-to-one conversations, which introverts can be great at, you can build a network of supporters within the company or organization. I'm a big believer in quality over quantity, so you don't have to be friends with everyone—in fact, you probably won't be—but it is very beneficial to make positive connections with a few people who will have your back. Sometimes, the only person you need on your side is your boss, just like we saw in our interview earlier with fellow introvert Fiona.

If you want to create a network of supporters beyond your boss, you might want to start off by thinking of one person in the company whom you "click" with the most. Get to know them better. You can invite them out to lunch, one-to-one. If they say something in a meeting that you agree with, back them up. Small gestures like these can go a long way. Also, pay attention to the connectors in the workplace—these are the people within the company who have a lot of connections and who have an ability to get things done. Figure out who or what is making the wheels turn, and what you can do to reach out and support these connectors.

Another interesting way of building relationships is by using the counterintuitive concept called the Ben Franklin effect. The Ben Franklin effect posits that if someone does you a favor, they will like you more. This theory originated with Benjamin Franklin, who wrote in his autobiography that he became friends with a legislator (who had petitioned against him!) by asking to borrow a specific rare book from the legislator's library. Franklin went on to write: "When we next met in the House, he spoke to me (which he had never done before), and with great civility; and he ever after manifested a readiness to serve me on all occasions, so that we became great friends, and our friendship continued to his death."[46]

A number of studies have corroborated Ben Franklin's experience. In one, participants were awarded money based on the number of correct answers they had given on a test. They were then placed into three groups. One group was asked by an unlikable researcher to do him a favor: the Psychology Department had run out of funds and the researcher was using his own money as payment for the winnings; so, could they give him his money back? The second group was not told this; instead, they were told by the secretary that the Psychology Department's funds were running low and were asked if they could return the money to her. The remaining third of the participants were not asked by the researcher or secretary to return the cash they had won. Interestingly, the participants who had done the researcher a favor rated him higher in terms of likability than the participants in the other two groups.[47] One theory on why this is the case is that people have an existing belief, an autofill, that they will only do favors for someone they like; thus, to maintain that belief, they will start liking someone after doing them a favor, even if they had previously disliked that person.

While I do not suggest you manufacture a way to ask someone for a favor simply so they will like you a little more, I hope you will keep this study in mind and let it affect how you work. If you've been meaning to ask a manager, coworker, or anyone else in the office for a favor (like providing you with honest feedback), but have been previously hesitant to do so, try it out and don't hold back.

Matthew Thought It Was All Due to Luck

Tall Poppy Syndrome isn't the only concept that can hinder self-promotion. Many introverts, as well as extroverts, also struggle with self-doubt when it comes to their work. They may downplay the quality of their work or strength of their skills, thinking "anyone can do what I do."

Matthew, a former client of mine, had a huge Instagram following that showcased his photography. He wanted to use that platform as leverage for gaining gigs for small corporations. Sounds like a useful situation for an artist, right? Except Matthew was convinced that most of his success on Instagram was due to luck.

He was afraid his fanbase wasn't following him because of his talent or his unique style; he feared they were only following him because of the pop-culture content in his photos. He was afraid that if he posted one photo that wasn't in his typical style, his following would disappear, and this fear stopped him from being his true self on his Instagram account and from reaching out to prospective clients.

I gave him homework: to listen to the audiobook *The Power of Vulnerability: Teachings of Authenticity, Connection, and Courage* by Brené Brown, and to create what's called a Smile File (I'll guide you through creating your own Smile File in a second). Two weeks after my call with Matthew, I checked in to see how he was doing. Part of his response is now in my own Smile File and is my phone's background image: "I am now owning my voice."

When doubt whispers in my ear, "Who do you think you are?" I am reminded to whisper back, "I help introverts own their power, and I have proof." It's time for you to find what you'll whisper back when self-doubt turns to you and speaks.

Creating a Smile File

I'm pretty sure that anyone who is not completely full of themselves or narcissistic has, at one time, felt like an imposter. At one point in your life, you may have felt like you were just making things up as you went along, and that a positive thing that has happened to you (like a promotion, an award, or getting hired) was a result of luck or an oversight. You may be worried that, any day now, the "Worthy Jury" will find you out. The Worthy Jury has examined your case, and they will announce to the world their verdict: that you are not worthy of whatever it is you've accomplished—that, instead, you are a fraud.

Imposter syndrome, a phrase coined in 1978 by Dr. Pauline R. Clance and Dr. Suzanne A. Imes, refers to the psychological phenomenon where one believes they are a fraud and will soon be found out. Imposter syndrome doesn't care who you are, and it doesn't care how much you have accomplished. Prominent people who have shared their struggle with imposter syndrome include beloved writer, poet, and recipient of a Presidential Medal of Freedom, Maya Angelou; Academy Award–winning actress Kate Winslet; and Neil Armstrong, the first person on the moon. While imposter syndrome doesn't just happen to introverts, since we very often turn to our own thoughts for answers, whenever we do get that "I'm an imposter" thought, it can stew and stew and stew, and end up creating a gaping hole in our self-esteem.

Imposter syndrome wants one thing—to keep you "safe." It considers you safe if you stay stuck and scared because of a fear of failure or a fear of getting hurt by the opportunities in your future. Imposter syndrome wants you to forget that you *are* strong and capable and deserving. The distinguished careers of Maya, Kate, and Neil prove that imposter syndrome doesn't know what it's talking about, and that it doesn't have to hold a person back.

One way to counteract imposter syndrome is to keep what's called a *Smile File*. A Smile File is a physical or digital file that contains external validation of your accomplishments and strengths.

When you feel imposter syndrome cropping up, look at your Smile File and remind yourself that your imposter syndrome cares about keeping you "safe" by keeping you scared. It's saying you're not worthy because it doesn't have access to your Smile File—the proof that you are capable!

Creating a Smile File just takes a few minutes:

Step 1: Decide if a digital or physical file folder works best for you. You'll want to keep your Smile File somewhere accessible so that you'll remember it exists whenever self-doubt starts to creep in.

Step 2: Create the folder on your computer or get out an actual file folder.

Step 3: Search around for great feedback that you have received from mentors, managers, and coworkers in the past. Include them in your Smile File. Copy and paste thankful emails, write down memories of uplifting conversations, and note down accomplishments (big or small). You can also include proof of those accomplishments—for instance, a copy of an award certificate or a screenshot of a report that shows growth or good sales.

Step 4: Keep that Smile File somewhere easily accessible.

That's it! A Smile File is a reminder that the negative thoughts and feelings you may have about yourself are not the objective truth. So please, please: put this activity on your to-do list for tomorrow—or put down this book right now—and make a Smile File!

And don't just create it and then forget it. It's something you should be continually adding to and updating frequently. Why not make it a monthly habit to update your resume *and* your Smile File on the same day? If your Smile File is regularly updated, you'll also have proof of recent accomplishments, which you can make use of when you ask for a pay raise or interview for a new job.

Fight, Flight, or Might?

If you were given free skydiving tickets, would you go? Most introverts I know would answer a big N-O!

If you have a sensitive self-preservation instinct, you might find yourself steering clear of seemingly scary or risky activities, even if they could have a huge positive effect on your life or career. Like asking someone out on a date, or asking your boss for a raise. I'm not going to encourage you to face every fear that you have, such as going skydiving; however, there are some challenges that are worth your while to take on. On the other hand, sometimes you'll experience a knot in your stomach that feels like fear, but is really your instinct telling you not to make an inauthentic decision just because an autofill tells you it's something you "need" to do. It's important to understand when you should ignore that feeling of fear, and when are the right times to listen to it.

When I try to figure out which fears to face, I turn to my three "fight, flight, or might" questions, which help me understand if I should avoid something that scares me or walk toward it:

- Is this fear preventing me from moving forward on a personal project, i.e., an important personal or professional goal?
- Is the goal something I truly want, or is it a goal I inherited from the culture I live in or from family or peer expectations?
- Can I achieve the same thing in a way that's more comfortable to me or in a way that's easier?

It's fairly common to feel pressured into a certain career. But being pressured by family, friends, culture, and coworkers into setting certain goals doesn't just happen at the beginning of your career; it can happen at any stage.

When Melinda came to me for help, she was considering applying to a more senior position at her company. Her boss expected her to take that promotion; after all, that's what you're supposed to want, right? You're supposed to always be "moving ahead" in your career, accepting more senior positions and higher pay, even if it means letting go of skills you had worked hard to cultivate. Melinda had gone to graduate school, had had numerous internships, and had spent thousands of dollars out-of-pocket on her professional development. She loved her job, and now she was expected to take a position that was mostly managerial and that would not allow her to use those skills she had honed. Plus, the previous person in that position had been subjected to extreme stress, and the thought of it all scared Melinda.

Melinda didn't want the job. And yet, "shoulds" swirled in her head. She "should" take the promotion—because you're supposed to take any opportunity to move on up. She "should" get the pay raise—because you're supposed to always want more money. She "should" take the opportunity to be the manager—because if she didn't, she might get a horrible manager instead.

When we spoke, I noticed that the reasons she had for considering taking the job were all fear-based, not want-based. She feared what the next manager would be like. She was afraid that not accepting the promotion would lead society to judge her because accepting promotions is seen as the "normal" thing to do. She was afraid that if she stayed in her current position, she wouldn't get a raise. On the other hand, she feared that if she were to take the job, it would most likely be at the cost of her mental health.

As the popular business coach and fellow introvert Marie Forleo says, "Everything is figureoutable." No matter what situation you're in, you can come up with a plan or a reframe—you can figure it out.

Melinda decided not to take the promotion, and together we planned how she would ask for a raise instead. And she got it—the biggest raise that year out of everyone at the company! The exercises on finding your why and the three "fight, flight, or might" questions above can help you discover what's worth fighting for and what's worth fleeing from. Everything is figureoutable, especially after you discover what it is you truly want.

Leaning into Fear

I'm a big believer in balance. As much as I dislike the idea that you always have to be stepping out of your comfort zone, as if constantly being afraid or uncomfortable is the whole "point" in life, I also think most people, at the end of their lives, regret prioritizing fear over their long-term happiness.

In an article on the "Top Five Regrets of the Dying," palliative nurse Bronnie Ware is quoted as saying that the fifth most common regret she hears is: "I wish that I had let myself be happier." As Ware explained in the article, "Many did not realise until the end that happiness is a choice. They had stayed stuck in old patterns and habits."[48]

> If you're like me, and it seems like you're afraid of nearly everything, the good news is that you have plenty of practice doing what scares you!

If you're considering doing something that scares you, here's an approach I call *Do-It-Scared* that I suggest to my clients:

- Observe
- Resolve
- Reframe
- Dip Your Toe In
- Jump In

Let's use Melinda as an example. She had to make a decision whether to apply for that promotion or stay in her current position. How did she get from "maybe I won't apply" to "I have decided not to apply"?

Observe: While "Just Do It" is certainly one approach to life, it's not the approach that works naturally for most introverts. Introverts are natural observers, and observation is a tool in our introvert toolbox that we use every day. Lean into that strength and take stock of the situation first. In her observation phase, Melinda focused on observing what she liked about her job and what she observed in the other managers at her company. This gave her the data she needed to make a guess about what it would be like to accept that promotion.

According to the Myers-Briggs Type Indicator, a popular personality assessment, there are two main ways of taking in information—focusing on the five senses and the here and now, or focusing on the big picture and possibilities. You probably do both, but lean one way or the other. It doesn't matter which way you prefer to take in information since there's no wrong way to observe. It's okay to mull over your options for a bit, as long as the temporary lack of a decision doesn't keep you unhappy and stuck. If you do find yourself very stuck, try using another method of taking in information. If you naturally focus on the here and now, spend a bit more time making informed guesses about your future self. If you tend to focus on the future, take a bit more time noticing your thoughts and feelings in the moment.

Resolve: After you observe, you will have to consider your options and make a decision. But what if each option you're considering scares you? For Melinda, the thought of taking the job scared her, and the thought of not taking the job scared her, too. If you're like me, you might go through the following five stages before you find the resolve to do the thing (or one of the things) that scares you:

1. Your brain will think about the problem rationally. It might see each side as logical outcomes. From an outsider's perspective, Melinda had good reasons to take the promotion, as well as good reasons not to take it. But for many introverts, the decision-making process doesn't stop at rational thought.

2. Your emotions kick in and you get scared of either possibility. Melinda feared that the new job would mean she would be under extreme stress; and she

feared that if she didn't take the job, she would get a new manager she didn't like.

3. After either looking at the data or checking in with your gut, depending on how you prefer to make decisions, you'll be leaning toward "I should just do it" or "this would be a big mistake." For Melinda, she already knew taking the managerial position was going to be "a big mistake," but something else was holding her back. The main reason she was still considering the position was so that she could get a pay increase, one that would put her at equal footing with her peers. She equated an increase in pay to feeling respected at work, which was very important for her. She was leaning toward a certain decision but still felt stuck.

As a life coach, I see this pattern with my clients 95 percent of the time: we *know* what we need to do, but fear tries to convince us that we can't or shouldn't act because we haven't discovered the "best" solution yet. Marie Forleo is really on to something . . .

> ## You can always figure it out.

Since Melinda's instinct said that taking the job would be a big mistake, instead of going against that instinct, we came up with a plan: she would turn down the position but still ask for a raise. It was a risk—she might not get the raise, and her new manager might be a nightmare. Was our plan the perfect "best" decision? We don't know. We don't have a crystal ball that can show us each path and help us to make the "best" decision. But if we do want to retain some control over our lives, we still need to choose—even if it's between two crappy options.

A lot of people, both introverts and extroverts, don't finish the Resolve phase because they are continually examining the data or checking back in with their instinct even though there is no longer any new information. They ignore what the data or their gut is already telling them, and they ignore the voice telling them to make a decision and move forward. The result is that they are stuck in indecision because there is no clear "best" decision in sight.

If you find yourself knowing what decision you should make, but are still stuck in indecision, then it's time to take action. This is the only point in the Do-It-Scared cycle where I try to be spontaneous, because if I don't quickly tell myself, "Okay, go!" and then take action, then I will talk myself out of doing anything scary but important. In her book *The 5 Second Rule*, Mel Robbins describes a similar approach that got her to make amazing changes in her life. She counts down *5-4-3-2-1-Go!*—and immediately acts when she reaches *go*. An introvert's home is in their mind, but to create change in our life, we also need to act.

Reframe. Just because something seems scary doesn't mean you have to keep thinking of it as scary. You can create a new reframe, a new autofill, that will help you get "scary" things done. This works on both a macro and micro scale. For instance, say you want to start doing public speaking because it will be good for your career, but you also hate the idea. First, take a look at what you want for your life—you know, those exercises you did at the beginning of this chapter: *Running into a friend* and *The* *perfect day.* Once you get a good idea of your goals from those exercises, you can start to create new reframes. Instead of having the thought "I'm terrified to do public speaking but I need to do it," turn that into something that's positive and true, such as, "I want to do public speaking because it will help me reach the role of my dreams." The key here is to make the reframe positive and truthful. Make your dreams bigger than your fears.

Reframing doesn't just work with general fears; it can also help with smaller disturbances. For instance, whenever I do public speaking, I always get a knot in my stomach beforehand. What I don't do is pretend like my emotions don't matter or shame myself into believing that "Everything is fine; just relax." Instead, I create a truthful reframe. Before I start speaking, I reframe my internal thoughts from "I am afraid" to "I am excited." Why does this work? Because, physically, fear and excitement feel very similar and manifest in the same ways—knots in the stomach, sweaty palms, etc. In a study by Alison Wood Brooks in the *Journal of Experimental Psychology*, she found that viewing anxiety as excitement actually helped and that it "increased the subjective experience of excitement and improved performance."[49]

If you could reframe something important to your career or life as exciting instead of scary, what would you reframe?

Dip Your Toe In. Taking action doesn't necessarily mean diving in headfirst so that you're suddenly submerged by the dark waters of fear. After all, if you wanted to become an Olympic swimmer, it would make sense to do some training first so you don't hurt yourself. Similarly, if you want to make it a goal to attend more networking events, you can begin by attending smaller events and then move on to larger ones later in the year.

If you want to do more public speaking, you don't have to start applying to do TED talks; start by going to a local public-speaking club, like Toastmasters.

And lastly, you **Jump In!** While you can keep dipping your toe in further and further until you're finally submerged, sometimes introverts prefer to jump straight in as soon as they realize their fears were unfounded and that they aren't going to drown. For some people, this is a reminder of the extent of their competence and power.

Sometimes it does make sense to do something that scares you.

Adopting a "Free Trait"

What if it's not just fear that's standing in your way? What if, in order to reach your goals, you need to be inauthentic for long periods of time?

In the book *Me, Myself, and Us*, fellow introvert Dr. Brian R. Little describes how people often have "core personal projects"—projects that have a considerable impact on that person's well-being, health, and career goals. When pursuing your "core personal projects," you may need to act in ways counter to your ingrained temperament. A debt collector who is usually a people-pleasing kind of person will sometimes need to put aside their usual state of behaving and be unforgiving if they want to keep their job. Dr. Little refers to these temporary periods of time where we act out of character as adopting a "free trait."

I think it's helpful to remember that most people, introverted or not, will find themselves in situations where they need to adopt a different way of behaving. Extroverted sales people might love chatting with potential customers and meeting new people, but at the end of the day, they need to stop connecting and sit down to create and send invoices to their new customers.

If you have to act out of character or "act like an extrovert" at work for temporary periods in the pursuit of a core personal project, consider thinking about those moments as you acting out your "free trait." It's a more forgiving phrase than if you think of yourself as acting inauthentically.

Introvert Success Steps for "Extroverting"

In certain situations, your "core personal project" may require some "extrovert moments," such as public speaking or attending in-person networking events. How do you confidently approach those extrovert moments? Let's look at the SPARK Method again:

S - SUPPORT

P - PREPARE

A - ACHIEVEMENT

R - RELEASE

K – KICKASS

S - Support: If you're friendly with an introverted coworker, ask them for help and support on how they've navigated such moments in the past. For instance, how did they get through their first presentation? Do they have any tips on attending networking events? If there isn't anyone you can turn to, go online. There are so many online communities out there, and you'll be able to find one that fits what you're looking for in terms of support. There are over one hundred Facebook groups for introverts that you can join, many of which are full of friendly people asking questions. And on Reddit, there are countless subreddits where you can ask questions. We're also lucky enough to be living in an age where countless articles have been published about being an introvert in the workplace. And, unlike seven years ago when I first started, there are many coaches and consultants out there who specialize in helping introverts.

P - Prepare: Yes, it's okay to prepare! For instance, if you're doing a presentation, practice that PowerPoint presentation and know your information inside-out. Your bosses should be able to tell that you know your stuff, compared to if you were just winging it.

A - Achievement: This is not the first time you've had to "extrovert." Focus on that time you went to a networking event and kind of liked it, or that time you did a cold call and got that sale. I'm sure you will find an example where you achieved something similar if you look back far enough. It doesn't have to be the same; just similar.

R - Release: Do you intensely dislike "playing the extrovert"? If you've thought it through, and resolved that playing the extrovert is the best course forward, release that frustration or anger—you don't have to hold on to it.

K - Kickass: Remember: you are, and will always be, resilient!

Flip the "Extrovert Switch"

Much like how actors frequently talk about having to "switch" between their characters and themselves, I believe that most introverts have an "extrovert switch" (and that most extroverts have an "introvert switch"). If I know I'm going to do some public speaking or will be attending a fast-paced meeting, I try to walk into the meeting room or onto the stage with my extrovert switch already on. When I have my extrovert switch flipped to ON, I'm a little quicker to respond (instead of taking the time to think something through) and a little chattier—which is not like my typical self.

Not sure if you even have an extrovert switch? Think of an extrovert you admire, and, in the comfort of your own home, try to emulate them. Try to walk and carry yourself like them—do you notice anything different? Try making a phone call where you conduct yourself like them. Did you speak differently? Pay attention: is there a certain feeling in your body or head that you normally don't have? When my extrovert switch is on, it feels like my brain is floating—like I have very little sense of self, but I also feel lighter and able to react to things that come my way a little more spontaneously, though in not quite the same depth.

Like streaming an eight-hour documentary on a smartphone, having the extrovert switch on constantly will be draining for your introvert batteries. Save it for the important situations where you need to be more extroverted. For most situations, your introverted strengths, such as listening deeply, will serve you well enough, but it is helpful to learn how to flip that extrovert switch when you think the energy drain will be worth it.

Remember the "Extroverting" Cycle

The SPARK Method (Support, Prepare, Achievement, Release, Kickass) I mentioned previously will prepare you for when it's time to flip on the extrovert switch. In addition to SPARK, you should also think about these four ways of managing your energy for the "extroverting" event if you want to minimize energy drain:

1. Gain energy

2. Microbreak
3. Regroup
4. Restore energy

If your event consists of speaking in front of a group of five friendly coworkers, the "Gain energy," "Microbreak," "Regroup," and "Restore energy" process may be very quick. But if you'll be, say, speaking at a large conference and you're scared of public speaking, the "extroverting" cycle will be longer.

Do something stress-free and relaxing the day before the event so you can **gain energy**. Right before your talk, take a **microbreak** and maybe a few deep breaths in the speaker room or the bathroom (and maybe skip that group lunch for the speakers to avoid an energy drain). After an extreme extrovert moment, many introverts find that they can't do anything afterward except stare at a wall for an hour or space out in front of Netflix—I consider this **regrouping**. And then comes the **restoration** part of the cycle. Take part in activities that will help you to relax. You could feel more restored after, say, a walk in a park, or maybe after doing some painting.

After you reach the end of the "extroverting" cycle and have restored your energy, you're ready to be your authentic self again!

Meditating Your Way Past Overthinking

It's 3:00 a.m., and you're still thinking about how you responded, "You, too," when your boss wished you happy birthday. Extroverts ruminate on mistakes they've made as well, but since our feelings are oriented inward, we introverts can find ourselves ruminating . . . and ruminating . . . and ruminating.

Meditation, the process of exercising your awareness, is an amazing practice for many introverts. There's a myth you might have heard that meditation helps you to control your thoughts, but that's not how I see it. For me, meditation helps me to *not* control my thoughts, to separate myself from my thoughts.

You may have heard of the classic psychological exercise where someone says to you, "Do not think of a polar bear," whereupon you'll involuntarily start thinking of one. This process is called *ironic process theory*. While you're thinking of a polar bear, you won't be able think of other things like, say, a hippo. Sometimes, actively trying not to think of something makes that very thought too big to ignore. The process of meditation asks you to simply let go of that thought of a polar bear. Energetically, there's a big difference between trying to force yourself to not do something, versus letting go of the hold that thought has on you.

Not too long ago, I fell into a months-long depression that included ruminating on painful events and ideas. I tried to force myself to stop thinking depressing thoughts, but that didn't work. What worked to get me into a clear enough mindset to realize that I needed to go to therapy was repeating to myself the words "present moment." I wasn't forcing myself to stop thinking depressing thoughts; I was redirecting my thoughts.

Let's say you're still thinking about that "you, too" comment you said to your boss. You may have tried telling yourself, "I need to stop thinking about what I said this morning," but perhaps that's not working (and from my personal experience, it rarely does). Instead, with the help of meditation, just let go of the thought.

Meditation is a way of giving your brain a pause button. It can train you to be in a state that is clear and relaxed. A huge benefit is that it helps you break the cycle of emotionally reacting to things. It's a fact that you said "you, too" to your boss. You can't change it. What you can change is whether you continue to ruminate on it. You can keep reliving the experience and cringe at past events in the middle of the night, or you can focus on so many other things instead, like your nice, soft pillow.

A common meditation technique often taught to beginners is to simply count your breaths from one to ten, and then start over and repeat again and again. If you find yourself miscounting or thinking about things, just start again from one. Other meditation techniques involve repeating a sound, word, or phrase, and focusing your attention on that. There are a number of free apps you can download that will help get you started. If one type of meditation isn't working for you, there are many other types of practices out there that you can adopt. Again, just do you! I really sucked at meditation at first, so be prepared for it not to click immediately.

If it doesn't seem like meditation is for you, you might want to look into meditation's close cousin, mindfulness. A quick definition of mindfulness is "being fully present." For example, feeling the softness of your pillow and the warmth from your blankets, rather than thinking about something that happened eight years ago. A simple exercise to bring yourself into the present moment is the "10-5-1" exercise. Note ten things you can see, then note five things you can hear (you might have to wait a minute for a new sound to appear), then note one thing you can smell.

If you'd like to read an introductory book to mindfulness and meditation, I recommend *Present Perfect: A Mindfulness Approach to Letting Go of Perfectionism and the Need for Control* by Pavel Somov. Another great resource for reducing anxiety is my friend

Andy Mort of AndyMort.com, who helps "gentle rebels" embrace their sensitivity. In his writing and on his "Gentle Rebel Podcast," he often talks about Stoicism, an ancient Greek philosophy that teaches you how to keep a rational mind in an unpredictable world.

Here's one last handy hint from Archbishop Desmond Tutu on redirecting your thoughts. Whenever he is awake and worrying in the middle of the night, he thinks about all the other people who are awake and worrying, too. And then he feels much better.[50]

Expert Introvert Corner with Lynn Dutrow, Courage Coach

Lynn Dutrow is a licensed clinical professional counselor, Courage Coach, and "Compassionate Ass Kicker" who loves to swear. In this interview she shares a simple step to reducing anxiety.

Thea: Is it normal to feel anxiety?

Lynn: Absolutely! Anxiety is part of our survival system. We all experience anxiety in some form or another.

Thea: At what point does anxiety become something negative?

Lynn: When we don't understand what Anxiety is telling us, we can perceive it to be dangerous or scary, when it may not be. Anxiety is a Protector, and, for some of us, it takes its job way too seriously and overdoes it!

Thea: How can we understand what anxiety is truly telling us?

Lynn: When we take a step back from perceiving Anxiety
as some amorphous all-knowing cloud (like a
dementor from the Harry Potter books), that's
when we can change our relationship with it.

Think of it like *The Wizard of Oz*. Dorothy and
her gang have been convinced by the locals that
Oz is all-powerful and all-knowing. They do his
bidding until Toto pulls back the curtain and
reveals the con man behind it. When I work with
clients who deal with anxiety, I teach them to put
a face to their anxieties and then figure out better
ways to interact with it so they can take back the
driver's seat from their worries. When they can be
their own boss and begin to change their relationship with Anxiety, that's when we start to understand and communicate better with it!

Thea: I'd love to hear an example of putting a face on anxiety.

Lynn: When I first started doing this work on myself, I
pictured my Anxiety like the blobby green Mucinex
"Monster" from the commercials. A bully who
"moved in" and took over at times. [Mucinex is a
cold and flu medicine, and they have a series of
commercials featuring Mr. Mucus, an animated
green blob that lives inside patients' chests.] I have
had clients picture Anxiety as "characters" like
Voldemort or the evil stepmother in Cinderella.

Once we have conceptualized Anxiety as a form (the technical term is *anthropomorphize*), then we can consider its backstory. For the stepmother: she thinks she is dependent on a man *and* has already screwed up both of her daughters, so she must actually be pretty insecure! Who is she going to try to boss around? The most competent person in the room—Cinderella! Once you anthropomorphize your Anxiety, it gives you "someone" to talk back to!

Thea: So, giving anxiety a face allows you to talk back to it versus seeing anxiety as this overwhelming feeling that's just everywhere?

Lynn: Exactly!

Thea: What else can introverts do to help ease anxiety?

Lynn: I noticed that you mentioned the phrase "ease anxiety" and would like to address that. One of the trickiest parts of working with people with anxiety (as well as dealing with my own) is that we often want to get rid of it or "ease" it. The best thing we can actually do is make it more challenging. Kind of like saying to Anxiety, "Is that all you got, b*tch?" One of the reasons that we are bossed around so easily by Anxiety is that we don't believe we are capable or competent enough. Being willing to do the hard things will help us to change our perception of ourselves around this issue of whether or not we are capable and competent.

Thea: Yes! Seeing ourselves as capable and competent is a big theme in this book. I think many introverts are taught the lie that they aren't capable of certain things, so they back away from challenging situations that involve things like leadership. It sounds like that same thing happens when it comes to our own thoughts. It's not just culture that's trying to convince us that we aren't capable enough; our own anxieties are telling us the same thing. And, like culture, anxiety is lying.

Lynn: Yes!

How We Talk to Ourselves

Negative self-talk is the negative story someone tells themselves about their potential and their state of being. If you've ever said a phrase like "I can't do this," you've experienced negative self-talk. Negative self-talk is normal in small doses—even if you feel like you don't have low self-esteem, you may still be susceptible to self-defeating thoughts. But you might find yourself having more negative self-talk when you're out of your comfort or effortless zone, making the task at hand even more difficult because you're also fighting your own thoughts.

Negative self-talk can occur in both introverts and extroverts, though I suspect that introverts who live in societies that value extrovert qualities are more prone to negative self-talk because we've internalized the lie society has told us—that we're not normal. Sometimes negative self-talk is an autofill learned from our parents and society at large, and sometimes it's a coping mechanism we teach ourselves. It can affect our outlook on any situation, how we show up in the world, and how others see us.

Negative self-talk becomes a problem when it starts to shape our view of reality and our ability to be happy. As clinical psychologist Nick Wignall wrote on his blog, "If our thoughts determine how we feel, that means how we habitually think will determine how we habitually feel."[51] In other words, frequent negative self-talk can have a very real and harmful effect on how we feel. If you want to feel happier at work, it may be helpful to take a look at what you say to yourself and try to determine if much of your self-talk is negative.

Negative self-talk can say many things about the work you produce. For example:

- I'm never going to finish this.
- I'm going to get fired because of this.
- This is a disaster.
- Why did they even ask me to do this project? Don't they know I'm not competent enough?
- I have no idea what I'm doing.
- Ugh, no wonder this happened. I always screw up.
- Why did I even think I could do this?

If you know you're prone to negative self-talk, you might want to seek out therapy. Additionally, being mindful and paying attention to the language you use can help, too. I suggest starting off with emails. For a few years now, whenever I remember to do so, I scan my emails to look for words and phrases that minimize my feelings, suggestions, ideas, and personal power. I've noticed that in emails where I make a request or statement, I often use words and phrases like "just," "only," and "I think." This kind of language is called *hedging*, which Wikipedia describes as a device that "allow[s] speakers and writers to signal caution, or probability, versus full certainty."[52] I often use words like "just" or "I think that maybe" even if I am certain about what I'm describing, or if I am writing to someone I can be direct with. You may notice this about yourself, too.

The way around hedging is to be more direct and not use words and phrases that undermine what you want to convey. For example, the phrase "I just wanted to suggest that we move the meeting to Wednesday because we're getting the next shipment on Tuesday" can be more powerfully phrased as "I want to move the meeting to Wednesday since we're getting the next shipment on Tuesday." When you use words like "I just wanted to suggest," the other person will think that you aren't confident about your suggestion. Hedging is so common that there's even a Gmail extension called "Just NOT sorry" that will highlight any "hedging language" when you're composing an email!

As I mentioned, negative self-talk isn't always a sign of low self-esteem. In the example above, my behavior may have been influenced (or autofilled) by how I've observed other women in American culture behave—not wanting to seem pushy and bossy. Whatever the case may be, know that if your negative self-talk is making you unhappy or affecting your work performance, it's okay to seek help and start making small changes in the way you communicate.

Understanding Energy

We've discussed how energy is one of the defining features of introversion, and one of the ways we're different from extroverts. Energy can refer to both our physical state and mental state. If you stay at a party for too long, you may become not just physically tired but also oh-my-goodness-don't-look-at-me-or-talk-to-me cranky. When we are very low on energy, things can become unpleasant for both us and the people around us, so it's important that you manage your energy effectively in the workplace. To do so, you have to understand what drains your energy and what recharges it.

You need to have enough mental energy to do great work for your boss. You also need enough energy to be nice to your coworkers (or at least to not get in fistfights with ones you don't like). You'll probably also want enough energy to be able to interact with members of the public and be a positive representative of the company, if that's part of your role. In short, I'm guessing you want to live your life with integrity, and making sure you balance your energy is a big part of that.

You may be familiar with the terms *night owl* and *morning person*. A morning person feels the most energized in the morning, while a night owl feels the most energized at night. While understanding these concepts will help manage your day-to-day energies, you likely also have an energetic rhythm and a change in mood or concentration between those morning and night hours.

I'm definitely not the first person to notice that energy and mood can change depending on the time of day. The humorous short story "Bartleby, the Scrivener: A Story of Wall Street," written by Herman Melville in 1853, takes place in the office of a mild-mannered lawyer. Two of the employees at the law office, Nippers and Turkey, are the exact opposite when it comes to their ability to focus on work. Turkey is great at his job in the morning, but after lunch he starts making mistakes and develops a bad temper. Nippers is distracted all morning, but after lunch he becomes productive.

Ask yourself when you do your best work during the day. Once you understand your natural work rhythm, you can plan your work around your daily energetic highs and lows. You can work smarter, not harder.

If you don't already know what time of day you tend to do your best work, try keeping an energy log. Grab a piece of paper and, every hour throughout your workday, note down:

1. The time
2. How you feel
3. What you are doing
4. Why you think your energy has changed (if it did)

Do this over a period of at least three days so you can start to see a pattern in your behavior. Sometimes, my clients say that "today" isn't a good day to start the exercise because today isn't a "normal" workday. But there will always be last-minute metaphorical fires you'll have to put out at any job, meaning there really isn't such a thing as a "normal" day. You'll still be able to learn from this exercise even if you do it on an "unusual" day. Once you've accumulated your three days of data, look for patterns. Do your energy levels drop at a certain time? Does a particular person or meeting drain you? Does any specific task *give* you energy?

Once you see patterns in your day, you can start to organize your tasks around these patterns. If you notice you are able to concentrate on creative tasks early in the morning, but that creative tasks drain your energy in the afternoon, schedule your work around that, if you can. Perhaps you can use your first hour in the office working on a big creative project, and then take time in the afternoon to check your email.

Just as important as discovering your productive times of day is noticing your unproductive times—and what you're trying to do during those moments. Does your energy log give you hints about whether you're more likely to complete tasks if you have had big stretches of uninterrupted time to focus on them? Or can you work in small chunks, but just need an hour of solitude during lunch?

You may also find that your energy changes depending on the day of the week. In an article in *Fast Company*, Jeremiah Dillon, the head of Market Insight & Strategy at Google Cloud, suggested to his team that Tuesdays and Wednesdays may be the peak of their weekly productivity[53] and the time when they should tackle their most difficult work problems.

You can also document your energy over the weekend. What tasks do you do on your days off that drain you or give you energy? If going to the supermarket on a Sunday afternoon feels exhausting, it might be worth it to go on a Friday evening or an early Sunday morning. Decide which works best for you—doing the chore on a weekday so that you leave your weekend with a bigger uninterrupted block of energy-uplifting time, or sacrificing sleeping in on Sunday so you can do your groceries when no one else is around. Just because you've done something a certain way in the past does not mean you have to keep doing it that way!

Once you understand how your energy ebbs and flows throughout the week and during the day, you can become more productive at work and feel more rested after your days off.

The Drain of Socializing

Now that you understand what drains you and what gives you energy, let's talk about socializing. Many introverts feel bitter about surface-level socializing, such as conducting small talk in the elevator, because they feel like they gain little from the interaction while still becoming depleted by it. Unfortunately, a lot of workplace friendships, or even just feelings of good will between coworkers, begin with these moments of small talk. If you feel like making small talk would benefit your long-term career plans or your short-term happiness in your job, you can actually be strategic about initiating small talk.

Let's think about a laptop computer. A full battery means you can unplug it from the energy source and take it anywhere. A full battery gives us the freedom to use our energy as we see fit. Instead of feeling bitter toward something that uses up your energy, try to remember that you've built up your energy so it can be used later for things that further your goals and happiness!

A great time to socialize may be when you're either energized or are generally unproductive. Do you naturally procrastinate once you get back from lunch? Maybe you can use this time to socialize with your coworkers since you're not going to get much done anyway. Or if you tend to be chipper in the morning, planning to start a conversation with a "hey, how was your weekend?" on a Monday, followed by an anticipated five minutes of patient listening, can go a long way to building a bond with a coworker and using your energy in ways that will count for a lot in the workplace.

Energy Drains into Energy Sustains

Some activities, which may typically drain your energy, have the potential to actually give you energy with a tweak here and there, or at least can turn out to be a neutral activity.

Perhaps you feel obliged to go out for drinks with your coworkers. Is there something you can do to make the experience a little less draining? Could you suggest a new watering hole that's less loud? Or maybe a comedy club with a two-drink minimum, which would satisfy both the group activity and the drinking requirement but also let you feel social without requiring you to talk too much?

One year, a coworker and I attended our office Christmas party, even though we both admitted to each other that we weren't looking forward to it. Though I dreaded the energy drain, I spent the evening laughing with my coworker at the absurdity of having a Christmas party with mandatory activities, and how interesting people act when they're drunk. It was a bonding experience for us, and I ended up having a great time. Pay attention to your energy drains, and have a think about ways you can minimize the drain and make that typically cringy experience into something that's at least a little fun.

Two Types of Downtime Activities

There are two types of downtime activities: *mindnourishing* and *mindnumbing*.

Mindnumbing activities are passive and require little thought and engagement. They tend to raise our energy levels mainly because they aren't taking energy away. TV is one example of a mindnumbing activity. On the other hand, mindnourishing activities require a little more energy input upfront, but they can create tons of energy at the end. For example, playing a musical instrument you're already familiar with can be a mindnourishing activity. Playing the ukulele requires you to get up, find the instrument, and tune it before you start, but once you get to playing, it can be a lot of fun. If you're trying to return to an old skill, such as getting back into painting after fifteen years, or if you're picking up a new skill, like knitting, you may find it a little draining at first. But once it stops being a struggle and starts being enjoyable, you could start to find it more energizing and more fulfilling than, say, Netflix.

Remember how we discussed that introverts have a different reward sensitivity than extroverts? If you're low on energy, you may say to yourself, "Playing the ukulele would require getting up off the couch, and I don't know if it's going to be worth it." While that sort of thinking may sound like laziness, it's actually just your difficulty in anticipating the rewards. My advice is whenever you have a little inkling that something might be fun, but you're not sure if it will be worth it, just give it a try anyway and do it for ten minutes! You might just find that those ten minutes will quickly turn into twenty.

Like the ebb and flow of your workday, you may also find it helpful to understand when are the right times to choose a mindnourishing or mindnumbing activity. After a long day, many introverts choose mindnumbing activities, like binge-watching Netflix (which I love), and there's nothing wrong with that! Being ashamed of how we spend our relaxation time is what I call *Downtime Guilt*, which is itself actually a source of energy drain.

> You can spend your downtime however you want; it's *your* time!

That said, if you feel like your weekend isn't fulfilling and you aren't fully energized enough at the start of the week, you may want to try adding more mindnourishing activities and see if that helps.

If you can't think of a mindnourishing activity, take a trip back down memory lane. Was there something you really enjoyed doing as a child? Did you love being outdoors, or did you mostly spend time alone inside doing something creative? What's something you used to do that you've stopped since you've become a busy adult? Try adding a little bit of that back into your life, maybe starting today.

Whatever downtime activity you choose, I hope you choose it guilt-free. The goal is for you to feel the most like yourself so you can stock up on the mental energy you need to live in integrity and show up in the world with authenticity.

"I'm always on the lookout for original content, news, innovative ideas, etc. Observing plays a major part in finding original content that many people tend to miss. I also do field reporting in different countries: photography, interviews, and written articles. So, I have to keep a close eye and pay attention to many details."

—José, director of communications, social media manager, and editor-in-chief of a magazine

V.

FINDING AND LANDING YOUR NEXT JOB

It was supposedly "the perfect company." People were playing a game of table tennis in the background, and a spontaneous meeting was happening under a large patio umbrella. But when Eleanor Shellstrop was offered a permanent position at the company, she turned it down. In the NBC TV comedy series *The Good Place*, we learn that the protagonist Eleanor used to be a rude, uncaring, and selfish person through a series of funny flashbacks. In this flashback, Eleanor is offered a permanent position after one year as a temporary worker, but she turns down the position because it isn't a good fit for her—she thinks it's weird that the coworkers hang out after work. After hearing this, the manager comments, "We all hang out because we're friends," to which Eleanor responds, "I know, it's weird."

That scene painted Eleanor as a rude introvert who isolated herself from others. It was a confusing scene for me when I first watched it, because I didn't even realize that a company with spontaneous meetings, table tennis, and hangouts after work was supposed to be the representation of the perfect job! Talk about an extrovert bias in the media! Sure, I want to be friendly with my coworkers, but I'm selectively social and I don't need to be friends with *all* of my coworkers or spend all of my time with them outside of work. I want to have a little fun at work, but I also want some psychological separation between work and play. Society's idea of a perfect job may actually be your nightmare.

When you begin job hunting, you may experience conflicting emotions—excitement and dread. It can bring up feelings of inadequacy, and it can also reveal cultural biases. You may think, upon discovering a so-called "perfect" job on paper: I *should* want this job; I *should* want to work in this company; I *should* want a bunch of coworkers who are friends and who hang out together all day long. And you might think: if this is the job I should want, why do I feel a sense of intimidation and dread? There are many reasons, authentic or inauthentic, why we might be attracted or repelled by a job, and it's no wonder that job hunting can be a confusing moment in your life.

In this chapter, we'll go over the various aspects of getting hired from an introvert's perspective. I want you to find a great job that fits *you*, regardless of whether the office has a ping-pong table or not.

Jobs Introverts Can Enjoy

As we've discussed, cultural autofills can determine how we react to the world around us and how we are treated by the people in our environment. So, it will probably be no surprise that autofills can also affect how you go about picking the "right" career.

I'm often asked the question, "What's the perfect job for an introvert?" I googled this question myself when I was thinking about a career transition and saw list after list of professions that didn't seem quite right for me. An issue with these sorts of lists is that they lump introverts into one category. However, if you recall from the first chapter, personality psychologist Jonathan Cheek and his colleagues created a theory stating there are four types of introversion—Social, Thinking, Anxious, and Restrained. Because there is such a wide variety of skills, interests, and personalities among introverts, it's hard for a list of introvert-friendly jobs to satisfy each individual's situation. Introverts are so varied that, as a group, we can enjoy and do well at any job, even one that involves considerable "extroverting."

I was curious if the stereotypes about "good" jobs for introverts would hold any weight in the real world, so I reached out to two introvert-focused Facebook groups and asked the following two questions:

"What job would be the least compatible with introversion?"

"If you love your job, what's your job title?"

Here are just a few of the over 150 responses I received:

What job would be the least compatible with introversion?	If you love your job, what's your job title?
Event/party planning	Event planning
Bartender	Bartender
Cold-calling sales	Salesman
Night club DJ	Professional square dance caller
Tour guide	Preschool bus driver
Retail	Assistant manager at a gas station

Customer service representative	Customer service
Call center	Call center
High school teacher	Teacher
Politics	Family service counselor at a funeral home
Radio show host	Flight attendant
ER nurse	Intensive Care Unit, clinical assistant

As you can see, many of the jobs that some people listed as not compatible with introversion were actually jobs that other introverts had and loved! Just because you're an introvert, it doesn't mean only a small number of careers are open to you. Introversion should only be one factor in your search for a great job.

Expert Extrovert Corner with Patrick L. Kerwin, MBTI Master Practitioner

Patrick Kerwin is author of the book *True Type Tales,* a collection of real-life stories about personality types in action in everyday life. Patrick is also a Myers-Briggs Type Indicator® Master Practitioner with over twenty-five years of experience working with healthcare, corporate, education, and nonprofit organizations to put the MBTI® instrument into practice for team-building, leadership development, and more. In addition to that, he's developed a tool called the KVS that helps people understand their career values. Patrick is also the only extrovert I interviewed for the "expert corner"; I thought it would be helpful to get an extrovert expert's point of view on the possibilities open to introverts.

Thea: You've been an MBTI consultant for over twenty-five years. What have you found to be the most common myth about personality and MBTI types in the workplace?

Patrick: Hands down the most common myth is that certain types are better at certain jobs than other types. One of the ways that the MBTI assessment gets horribly misused is when people are told that they should do certain jobs based on their type, or that they shouldn't do other jobs based on their type. Using the MBTI assessment in that way mistakes preferences for skills or proficiency, and people can have or develop skills outside of their MBTI preferences. Sometimes people don't even fully understand what a personality preference really is, like in the case of introversion. They attach certain kinds of characteristics to introversion that actually are not part of the Jungian framework and the MBTI framework of introversion.

Thea: Should an introvert, or an extrovert, avoid applying for a job that doesn't seem to fit their personality type?

Patrick: That's a tricky question because the answer is: it depends. Sometimes people think that they're going to be dissatisfied if their job doesn't "match" their personality type, and that's not necessarily true. For example, some of the introverted

physicians I work with in the physician leadership programs I conduct are on the go so much
that they don't have time for introversion and
describe being burned out. But other introverted
physicians I work with actually do have time here
and there to reflect and catch their breath, and
they are quite satisfied. So, for introverts, if a job
is going to require a lot of outer focus that could
be draining, you have to ask yourself, "How am
I going to get my introverted needs met so I can
continue to thrive at my job?"

The flip side applies to extroverts. If you're
considering a job in an environment where you'll
need to be focused inwardly, and you know that
you're not going to have a lot of interaction with
people, that doesn't necessarily mean that job
will be a bad fit. But you'll want to ask yourself,
"How will I get my extroverted needs met?"
For example, will you be able to take the time
to socialize with others during the day or get
involved in a group project or a club at work?

The other reason "it depends" is because
when people are making these career decisions
and looking for a good fit, they need to consider
more than just their personality.

Thea: What else should people be considering when
they're looking at career options?

Patrick: I'm a believer that career values are the first filter for determining if a job is going to be potentially satisfying for you. If a job doesn't meet the things that you really want out of work, whether it's meaning or money or creativity or whatever career values you have, then that will be a barrier to your career satisfaction regardless of your personality type. The moral of the story is that when you're evaluating a job, there are additional factors to consider besides personality.

Thea: What else should introverts consider when looking for a job?

Patrick: The trick is to look for careers or opportunities where your career values, your personality, your interests, and your skills all intersect. Those are the sweet spots to investigate.

Thea: Can introverts excel in leadership roles?

Patrick: Absolutely. I have lots of examples to support this since most of my work is in leadership development. I have worked with many, many introverts who are outstanding, effective, and inspirational leaders. But sometimes people confuse introverts as being misanthropic or not liking people.

But introversion is simply about your source of energy. A lot of introverts enjoy interacting with other people, and introverts don't always have to or want to work alone. What's key for an introvert is being able to regulate when you do interact and when you don't.

The Tale of Three Introverts

For some introverts, minimizing energy drain may be one of their primary reasons for pursuing a certain career. For other introverts, there are more important factors than maintaining a full tank of energy. For instance, one factor may be feeling like they are part of a bigger cause; another may be having the ability to work with their hands. Let's take a look at the career progression of three introverts and how they discovered which factors were important to them in a career.

My friend Margaret thought she was going to become a professional tutor. Tutoring was her first job in college, and she was good at it. Plus, she found meaning in helping others succeed. But when she pursued a job as a tutor, she discovered that the pay wasn't great, and her energy was completely drained at the end of the day. To address those issues, Margaret could have started her own business and charged more money; she could have taken on fewer clients; she could have started a system to weed out the most draining customers. But at the end of the day, she realized a career in tutoring didn't provide her with enough gratification to be worth the energy drain. She now works in a technical profession that involves minimal interactions with others, but volunteers as an ESL (English as a Second Language) teacher for two hours each weekend.

Tina thought she was going to be a film editor. Growing up in Los Angeles, she watched countless movies and TV shows as a kid, graduated with a degree in media studies, and interned at the production studios of a famous celebrity. Tina knew she was an introvert and didn't want a job that required her being around tons of people in the glitzy movie scene. Plus, she loved it when her college classes required editing, so becoming an editor just seemed like the next logical step. But something was missing. Tina is an INFJ—in Myers-Briggs Type Indicator talk, that means she's an introvert who looks at the big picture, strives for harmony, and avoids last-minute stress. She may have been good at editing, and the job would certainly have suited her introversion, but based on her Myers-Briggs Type, and after thinking about what she did during her free time in college (organizing campus events), she realized that being a full-time editor wouldn't be fulfilling. She later found herself pursuing a career in college counseling for high school students, which eventually led to being a coach for introverts and a facilitator for workshops about the difference between introversion and extroversion. The work she does now may be more draining than that of a film editor, but she has a great deal of independence and fulfillment, and seeing the positive changes in people's lives feels worth the drain. Tina, by the way, is my Starbuck alias (what I call my *nom de coffee*), which I use because I don't see the point in extending my interaction with baristas just to spell out my real name.

Steven, whom I first connected with online while doing research for this book, had different reasons for seeking a career change. Steven currently works in a warehouse, driving forktrucks across huge warehouses and driving the company truck between plants. He likes his work, but the ingrained culture of the factory floor really doesn't suit him. Steven, who previously worked as a team lead in another company, says, "The factory life is me, and I get it." He doesn't want to change fields entirely.

Instead of leaving the warehouse life, or feeling inauthentic by trying to assimilate to the factory floor culture (previous attempts to change the culture had landed him in trouble), Steven is now working on getting a CPIM—Certified in Production and Inventory Management—so that he can transition into the administration side of the manufacturing industry.

While Margaret, Steven, and I have very different jobs, the common theme is that we're all pursuing a job that fits our unique personality and needs. What may be important to you may not be important to another introvert. Yes, our introversion and energy management is key, but it doesn't have to be the only factor when thinking about what jobs to pursue.

Follow Your Passion?

"Follow your passion." How many times have you heard that advice? Sounds great in theory, right? It seems like if you follow your passion and do the *one* thing you're apparently meant to do in this world, you'll always love your job.

If you look up *passion* in the dictionary, you'll see it defined as something along the lines of "an irresistible emotion." If you consider yourself a person motivated by logic, the idea that you should find a job that leads to the loss of control might sound like your worst nightmare. You probably want to be in control of your job rather than have your job control you! Plus, building a career around your passion may be the source of immense energy drain, especially if you can't separate it into a clear work-life balance. If you can't walk away from a job at the end of the workday because it's irresistible, how are you going to recharge your energy? By finding a career that you're not madly passionate about but that you enjoy, that fits your interests, or that suits you in other ways, you'll be giving yourself the crucial ability to recharge your energy once you've clocked in your hours.

The "find your passion" concept may have started off with good intentions, but in this day and age, it has done more harm than good. While I love the idea that we should try to align much of our life around our values and interests, I've coached introverts who were in agony simply because they couldn't find their passion or align it with their career.

It's an agony I'm familiar with. I've been one of those people who have had days (okay, months) of distress because I couldn't locate this so-called passion. I used to look at people like Elizabeth Gilbert in envy—she'd always known she wanted to be a writer, and she has since accomplished that and more with the bestselling *Eat, Pray, Love*. In those dark moments, I would think: *If I'm an introspective and fairly self-aware person, why can't I think of the one career I was meant for?!*

Even if you are clear on what your passion is, I don't think it's necessary to align it with your job. You can still be a happy, fulfilled person by pursuing your passions and interests outside of work. A construction worker who isn't passionate about construction but who is obsessed with dogs can still find meaning in his week by volunteering at the local animal shelter on the weekends or the evenings. Simply put, the construction worker who likes his job but who isn't driven or controlled by it can walk away at the end of the day to connect with his other interests. Do you really want a career you're so passionate about that it becomes all-consuming and stressful, even outside of your working hours? Instead, you can "pursue your passion" on your time off to help recharge your energy, so that when Monday morning comes rolling around, you can return to a job you enjoy.

Pursuing your passion outside of work may come in the form of volunteering or through a side hustle (a business that's designed to generate a little extra income as you work in a full-time job). If you want to learn more about side hustles, I suggest reading Chris Guillebeau's book *100 Side Hustles: Ideas for Making Extra Money*—the hundred businesses mentioned in the book will provide you with a wealth of inspiration and ideas for making a bit of extra money in a way that might involve your interests.

So, if you haven't found your one true "passion," that's okay! You can still have a fulfilling career or a job you like and be working in a field that excites you without being boxed in by a passion.

Expert Introvert Corner with Beth Gea, Coach for Multipotentialites

What if, instead of not being able to find any passion, you can't choose between your many passions? Beth Gea is an introvert who knows what it's like to be interested in many different fields. She's a multipotentialite, which means she has many interests and doesn't consider herself to have one true calling. While originally from Spain, she now lives in Japan where she pursues her many interests, including coaching other multipotentialites who are having a hard time adjusting to cultures that think everyone should become experts in one field.

Thea: What is a multipotentialite?

Beth: A multipotentialite is a person who doesn't have
a "one true calling" because she has many. She's a
fast learner driven by curiosity, a divergent thinker,
and is able to find new ideas in the intersections
between completely different fields of thought.

Thea: What are the top strengths of being a
multipotentialite?

Beth: We are creative thinkers and quick learners
because we are used to learning new things. We
are passionate about whatever interests us in a
particular moment and have a desire to share
it with the people around us—we like to teach
people. We are divergent thinkers, and we can
make connections between different fields that
perhaps no one else has thought of because of our
background.

Thea: What do you think about the phrase "find your
passion"?

Beth: Ugh! Multipotentialites will think: *How am I supposed
to find my one true passion when I have soooo many?*

Thea: What should a multipotentialite do instead of
worrying about finding their one passion?

Beth: When I work with my clients, we focus on the ideas
and projects that they are passionate about in the
moment; then we look at their current needs. One
thing we need to understand is that being a multipotentialite is a way of living and existing in the world,
and that we don't have to fit every aspect of our jobs.
We may be fortunate to have a job that has variety
and that challenges us and makes us feel as if what
we do is important (like my current job!). If a job is
not as varied, we compensate it with our hobbies, a

side hustle, or voluntary work. One thing that many multipotentialites face is lack of steady income due to the fact that many of us often quit jobs.

Thea: How should a multipotentialite approach searching for a job?

Beth: For a multipotentialite to be happy in a job, first of all, it has to be the kind of job where the values of the workplace are similar, or at least not completely different than, her own. She also has to feel that the job is important to her, and that it is doing some good to the community. This doesn't have to mean "saving the world"—I have a client who is an electrician and who likes his job because he feels that his work keeps people safe in their homes.

Thea: Is there anything we didn't cover that you would like to mention?

Beth: One thing multipotentialites have to be aware of is their mental health. Since there are so many things that we want to do and not enough time to do them all simultaneously, we can feel anxious or depressed very easily. It is a good thing to have tools and techniques at hand to deal with these feelings. Another thing is to be aware that all of our passions have a life cycle and that eventually most of them are going to end the cycle and "die"—and that is okay. Even if a passion or idea "dies," we can plan to take with us what we have learned and apply it to something else we are doing. Or find a variation of the same passion.

Exploring Your Career Options

When faced with the same pieces of information, two people can come to two very different conclusions. Some people spend more time thinking through the here and now, while other people focus on future possibilities. Some people tend to rely more on their heart (their values), while others rely or their head (the facts in front of them). When you need to make an important decision, like what job to pursue, why not use a variation of decision-making methods to come to a conclusion? I suggest taking this in-depth multi-pronged approach to career exploration before you begin applying for jobs:

1. Innie-storming
2. 1k question
3. Gathering data
4. Personality match
5. Gut check
6. Verify

1. Innie-storming

Oftentimes, very logical introverts can get into a career-exploration rut because they reject each career that doesn't suit their every need. Other times, very creative introverts might be overwhelmed by the infinite possibilities of prospective careers and don't get past the dreaming stage. If you see yourself in either of these camps, or somewhere in between, it's time to take the first step in finding a new career: innie-storming, or brainstorming, introvert style. Here's how you innie-storm possible careers:

Step 1: Get a piece of paper and a pen, or open up a spreadsheet program.

Step 2: Create six columns.

Step 3: On the top of the first column, write "Jobs." In this first column, you'll be doing what's called a "brain dump," which means dumping out all of the ideas in your head and onto a piece of paper.

Step 4: Think of a career, industry, or job title that sounds mildly interesting to you, and write each of those jobs down on separate rows in the first column.

Step 5: Repeat Step 4 until you have at least ten to twenty jobs you are at least a little interested in. That's it!

It's okay if the jobs or industries don't seem like practical career choices, or if you aren't sure you'll actually like the job—at this stage you're just writing down a bunch of ideas. Did you want to be an astronaut when you were a kid? Write it down. Do you really love the title "Chief Happiness Officer" but have no idea what it means? Write it down. The goal is to get ideas out of your head and onto a piece of paper. We'll edit the list in the next section.

2. The thousand-dollar question

The online retailer Zappos has an ingenious method of separating the new employees who are truly excited about working there and the ones who just want to take home a paycheck. During the middle of their four-week training experience, new employees are presented with "The Offer." "The Offer" is this: stay an employee of Zappos, or quit now and you'll be given a thousand dollars. Each new employee is basically bribed with a thousand dollars to quit before the training ends.[54] I think this is a brilliant way to create a workforce of employees who are enthusiastic about the company and who want to work at Zappos more than they want a quick buck (or a thousand). For each new employee that quits, Zappos is technically down a thousand dollars, but it doesn't have to spend extra effort training an employee who isn't emotionally invested in working there and might quit soon anyway.

You can use "The Offer" as a thought experiment to help you decide if there are any jobs on your innie-storming list that aren't interesting enough for you to finish a four-week onboarding process.

Step 1: Look at the first job you wrote down on your innie-storming list (you can skip the jobs on the list that are vague or that are just general names of certain industries).

Step 2: Imagine that you got that job, and a week into your employee onboarding process, you had to choose between keeping the job or taking a thousand dollars to leave. Which would you choose—continuing the training process or quitting? In order for this exercise to be effective, you should assume that you don't need that money right away.

For instance, perhaps the first job on your list is an astronaut. You may have loved the idea of being an astronaut as a kid, but as an adult, you can't fathom being away from your family for so long; plus, you're claustrophobic. In that case, after a week of training, you'd probably already want to quit, and the extra thousand dollars would be the icing on the cake. Again, this step is not the time to think about the practicality of starting a career in that field; we're just eliminating jobs that are obviously a bad fit.

Step 3: If you can't picture wanting to work at that job more than wanting to be paid to quit, cross it off the list. If someone would have to pay you much more than a thousand dollars to pass on the opportunity, keep the job on the list. We're trying to find a job that you can commit to, that will be a good fit, and that you're excited about.

Step 4: Repeat steps two and three for each job on your innie-storming list.

By the end of this exercise, hopefully, you should have crossed off about half of the jobs from your long list of possibilities. If you haven't crossed off about half yet, identify up to ten jobs/careers that seem like they would be a good fit for you, circle them, and focus on the circled jobs in the next few exercises.

3. Gathering data

Next, we'll gather data on each of the remaining jobs. If you're about to do research on one of the jobs on your list, but it doesn't even seem worth the few minutes of research, that's probably a red flag that you're not very interested. If this is the case, cross the job off your list.

Step 1: At the top of the second column, write "Salary." At the top of the third column, write "Job requirements." And at the top of the fourth column, write "Notes."

Step 2: Look up the job online and note an estimated salary in the second column. In the United States, the US Bureau of Labor Statistics is a reliable source for this information, as are for-profit websites that collect salary information.

Step 3: Next, look online for that position's job requirements. For instance, perhaps the job will require a certain degree, skill, or specific training. Write these down in the column "Job requirements."

Step 4: Under the fourth column "Notes," write down any other pertinent information you found while doing your research.

Step 5: Repeat steps two to four for each job on the list that isn't crossed off or that you've circled.

4. Personality match

Next, label column five "Personality match." You'll be looking through each of the questions below and coming up with a general "personality match" rating for each remaining job, with one being the lowest and ten being the highest match.

  a. How will this job affect my energy levels?

  b. Do I expect that I'll have enough downtime after work to recuperate from the energy drain?

  c. Do I expect to like at least some aspect of the job 80 percent of the time? It is highly unlikely that you'll love your job 100 percent of the time or find a job that fulfills 100 percent of your needs and desires—that job likely does not exist. Instead, aim for enjoying your job at least 80 percent of the time. That may sound like a random number, but it's actually taken from the 80/20 rule, also known as the Pareto Principle, which states that 80 percent of results comes from 20 percent of its causes.

    d. Is there an expectation in this career that I'll be able to use my introverted qualities (for example, the focus necessary in computer programming) most of the time, or that I would have to spend a lot of time "extroverting" (for example, the gregariousness required in customer service)?

    e. Does the job allow me to work with my strengths (whatever your individual strengths are, such as math, writing, or working with your hands)? Or would I be spending a lot of time compensating for my weaknesses?

    f. Does this job match my values and interests?

5. Gut check

On the top of column six, write "Gut check." Then, look at all of the information you've written in the previous columns. In column six, for each job you haven't yet eliminated, rate it on a scale of one to ten based on your gut feeling, with one being the weakest and ten being the strongest. To measure gut feeling, you can use criteria you normally think about when you're considering applying to a job—how "interesting" or "fulfilling" it seems. You can also take into account practical criteria like "Salary" or "Job requirements."

6. Verify

It's time to narrow down the list even more!

    Step 1: Look through the new information you have filled out in columns two to six and cross off the jobs that really won't fit you.

Step 2: Examine the jobs you just crossed off—do they give you an idea of a better-fitting job in the same field? Perhaps you're unwilling to go through the training necessary to become an astronaut, but you could look for work at a company in the aerospace industry. Write down any new job ideas that might suit you better, and do the same process of research, etc., for each of these new job ideas.

Step 3: Continue going through the list and narrow down your options. You want to eventually whittle the list down to five items.

Step 4: If I asked you to email strangers working at any of these jobs to conduct informational interviews and ask them questions about their work, would you do it? If someone couldn't pay you enough to have a brief email conversation with a stranger about the job in question, or if it just doesn't seem worth that extra effort for you, it's a sign to cross it off.

Step 5: Narrow the list down to three possible jobs.

Step 6: Conduct an informational interview with one person in each job. If you're an anxious or reserved introvert, this might freak you out, but it's really important to get a sense of what the job is *really* like instead of just reading about it online. I've done many in-person and email informational interviews, and I've found the key to a good interview is to find out the little day-to-day details about that job. For instance, you could ask:

- What do you like most about your work?
- What do you like least about your work?

- Do you often work overtime?
- What's it like working with the job's key players? (For instance, if you're thinking about working in a warehouse, ask about how the drivers treat warehouse workers.)
- Do you have a lot of autonomy in your work?
- Is this job what you expected it would be?
- If you could do it all over again, would you still choose this career?

Note that the answers you receive from these interviews will be relevant only to a specific work environment, and they may be from the point of view of someone with a different personality to you. But you can still glean very important information. In the past, I've decided not to go with a certain type of work environment based on an informational interview. Another tip: some of the questions I listed above are personal in nature, so I would only recommend going into the deeper emotional questions if you sense a strong connection during the interview, or else it could get awkward very fast.

Once you've done your informational interviews, you should have a *much* better understanding of which career(s) might be a good fit for you.

Just Tell Me What Career to Pick!

I completely understand if you skipped through all of the exercises above and are just looking for a list of jobs that require little social interaction! I have a few ideas for you:

- Animal Care (dog walker, pet sitter, etc.)
- Transportation (delivery, long-haul, cab service, etc.)

- Finance (accountant, bookkeeper, auditor, etc.)
- Computing (software developer, web developer, programmer, etc.)
- Transcription (legal, medical, etc.)
- Technical (medical technician, lab technician, etc.)
- Mechanical repair (auto, electrical, industrial machine, etc.)
- Writing (freelance, proofreader, technical, etc.)

Find a job you enjoy—80 percent of the time. Pursue contentment. Pursue interests. Pursue fulfillment—in either your work or your leisure time. And remember that if the advice to follow your passion has left you in agony, then maybe it's time to reexamine what you're searching for in a new job.

Tapping into Your Network

You've probably heard that tapping into your network is an important part of the job-hunting process. This can be depressing for introverts to hear—we just aren't as social as extroverts, and therefore we also tend to have smaller networks. But a comparatively smaller network does not mean an ineffective network.

You may have heard of the terms *weak ties* and *strong ties*. A weak tie is an acquaintance, someone with whom you may occasionally interact but aren't close to. You can greet a weak tie by name, but you wouldn't ask them to help you move. A strong tie is someone whom you're close to, like a family member, good friend, or coworker. Your strong ties exist in separate "bubbles"—there are likely people in your "family bubble," "tight-knit group of friends bubble," and "team at work bubble." Each person in the bubble knows each other, but they often don't know the people in your other bubbles.

Counterintuitively, it has been found that strong ties are actually less important than weak ties when networking for a job.[55] This is because weak ties can tap into their own bubbles, which are filled with people you don't already know. They are the bridges that provide access to new bubbles and different people whom you may have previously struggled to reach. Plus, you probably also have more weak ties than strong ties. Your stronger ties may work harder to help find you a job, but when you look at the bigger picture, your weak ties have a larger network of people they can access. When it's time to explore career options, reach out to your strong ties first, and then quickly move on to your weak ties.

You probably have more weak ties than you think. Even small points of connection can be powerful. When strengthening your network, either in preparation for or during a job hunt, reach out to:

- Long-lost friends
- Old coworkers
- Former classmates
- Favorite teachers
- Fellow members of associations
- Connections from hobbies, volunteering, or religious institutions
- If you've been to college, members of the alumni/ae association

You can find most of these contacts on social media sites like Facebook or LinkedIn. Also, don't discount Twitter or Instagram weak tie connections. I've done many favors for acquaintances I've met on Twitter and have asked for many favors as well.

Invite Serendipity for Coffee

Remember that introverts have a different approach to seeking rewards than extroverts. We often don't get excited by the idea of networking because it's hard for us to know if our "extroverting" effort will be worth it. In other words, when it comes to networking, it can be easy to discount reconnecting with a weak tie because it's difficult to predict whether a weak tie will help or if we're just wasting our time and energy.

Let's say you are hoping to land a job with Google. You've asked your strong ties, and they haven't been able to help. So, you start thinking about your weak ties and decide to ask your hairdresser. It may seem unlikely that your hairdresser in New York would know someone working at Google in California, but you literally never know. Even if your hairdresser doesn't have a direct contact, she might be able to put you in touch with one of her strong ties—her sister-in-law who works in Silicon Valley, where Google is headquartered.

In other words, invite Serendipity for coffee. Serendipity refers to the positive events that happen by chance. We never know if Serendipity will show up, or if our actions will lead to a dead end. All we can do is invite Serendipity by choosing to act versus avoid. Sure, Serendipity might decline the coffee date because she's too busy, but if she accepts, you might find yourself with a lead for a great job. If you don't extend an invitation simply because you're afraid it might not work out, then it'll *certainly* not work out. Yes, reconnecting with people can take time and energy, but your future is worth the effort.

Facebook is an excellent place to start reaching out to weak ties once you've already asked your strong ties for help. But before you start reaching out to "Facebook friends," I recommend doing a few things first:

1. Clean up your profile. Take down any posts or pictures that are unprofessional.
2. Look through your public posts for anything inflammatory and delete them.
3. Set your privacy settings to *Private* so friends can't tag you in embarrassing photos.
4. Fill out your profile; for example, your job history.
5. Start occasionally posting positive things that are related to your career (such as articles).

Then, start reaching out! Again, don't be afraid to invite Serendipity to the table. You may be tempted to skip Alejandro, the biomechanical engineer from the Congolese drumming class you both took at the local community college last summer, because you two work in very different fields, but he has connections that you don't, and one of them may be just the person you were looking for!

When reconnecting with someone, don't be afraid to ask directly for help. It might be easy to say something vague like, "Hi, I'm looking for a job in accounting, can you let me know if you hear anything?" But the person on the other end of that message probably won't just "hear of something." Instead, ask if they know of anyone who works at certain companies or if they have any contacts in the area or field you want to work in.

If the person you're reaching out to knows of someone, please follow through and connect with that contact! I've seen many introverts put out the call for help, only to allow their courage to disappear and neglect to follow through. This is counterproductive and can make you look unprofessional (and ungrateful) to the people who were trying to help you.

Since energy is important to introverts, we often make guesses about whether we think we'll get a good result from our efforts, and then make decisions based on those guesses. But remember that we just can't predict where a conversation or a job lead will take us. A great lead may go nowhere, and a seemingly random lead that doesn't seem worth the effort can bring you exactly to where you need to be. Serendipity is waiting to hear from you . . .

Should I Apply?

Let's say you do find the almost-perfect job or the almost-perfect company; however, you still have some hesitations about applying for the position. Maybe it's a few more miles than you want to drive. Maybe you would be working in a company that's bigger or smaller than you're used to. Or maybe you only fit part of the job requirements . . .

A survey by Tara Sophia Mohr, author of *Playing Big: Find Your Voice, Your Mission, Your Message*, asked the question: "If you decided not to apply for a job because you didn't meet all the qualifications, why didn't you apply?" The majority of respondents cited their reason as: "I didn't think they would hire me since I didn't meet the qualifications, and I didn't want to waste my time and energy." Mohr's interpreted the results as such: "They thought that the required qualifications were . . . well, required qualifications. They didn't see the hiring process as one where advocacy, relationships, or a creative approach to framing one's expertise could overcome not having the skills and experiences outlined in the job qualifications."[56]

Having worked as an HR assistant in a publicly traded company, and as the person who sorted through job applicants in two other positions, I can tell you that a list of job requirements should be seen more as a wish list than a checklist for many positions. Most likely, one of the primary things the hiring manager will look for is an indication that you actually want the job.

> Think of the job requirements as more of a wish list than a checklist.

Career coach Ellen Fondiler, who spent ten years as the director of a nonprofit, agrees. In an article on the career website *The Muse*, she's quoted as saying: "The people I ultimately chose to hire were not always the 'most qualified' or the 'most experienced.' They were the people who demonstrated genuine enthusiasm for the organization and our mission. Skills can be acquired. But enthusiasm is either there—or it's not.'"[57]

Don't let the fact that applying for jobs can be tedious or that you may not be 100 percent qualified stop you from pursuing what seems like a great opportunity! Invite Serendipity for coffee.

Expert Introvert Corner with Meredith Tseu, Career Coach at MLT Careers

A fellow introvert and a certified Global Career Development Facilitator, Meredith Tseu has been running her own career coaching business since 2008. "Love Mondays again" isn't just her business's slogan—she's genuinely passionate about helping people find the job and the job-hunting approach that feels authentic.

Thea: Do you find there's a difference between your introverted and extroverted clients?

Meredith: My introvert clients often research their potential employers more and work harder on their resume, cover letters, or LinkedIn profiles. But too much research before deciding where to apply, for instance, can backfire.

Thea: How can researching too much backfire?

Meredith: Spending a lot of time on search engines and online applications, and less time networking, either in person or through social media, may backfire.

Thea: I'm assuming that an introvert who thinks they have a small number of connections shouldn't just discount their network. How can introverts tap into their existing contacts?

Meredith: The first step is to share that they're job hunting and give specifics on what they are looking for. This can be done privately by email. Ask for information—any jobs they should know about or any companies they should consider, instead of simply asking for someone to recommend them.

They also shouldn't forget about the wider networks they're a part of—alumni groups, especially. Even if you didn't know a fellow alum personally, a lot of times that connection can be meaningful enough to open doors, especially if you studied the same subject.

Thea: How can an introvert make job interviews less stressful?

Meredith: First, I do think job interviews can be really stressful these days for introverts. Many of my clients go through three to five rounds of interviews for a position. And many of those interviews have a group dynamic, like a panel question period.

I'm a big fan of meditation apps for practicing breathing exercises. Conscious breathing is invisible during an interview but can really help you re-center when you get a tough question or just get "peopled out" halfway through a long interview.

Introverts can also practice talking about themselves out loud, with a person or even just with a video function on their phones. They can rehearse answers and even time themselves to get a feel for a two-minute answer, for instance. Many times, I practice mock interviews with clients and they'll think they've talked too long—but I time their answers and it's not too long even if it feels like it!

Thea: I can definitely understand misjudging how long you've been talking. Do you have any tips for interviews with a group dynamic, where multiple candidates are being interviewed at the same time? Or interviews with a panel questions period?

Meredith: Group interviews with multiple candidates can get chaotic, and it can be easy to feel off balance. Using active listening skills can impress interviewers, so listen to fellow candidates and reference something they've said, then build on it. It can show that you're team-oriented, thoughtful, and respectful at the same time.

Another thing to be aware of is body language, which can be tough to remember when many people are speaking/engaging. The basics, like eye contact for example, can be much more complicated in a panel interview. Look out for including someone who is calling in to the interview from off-site, either on an intercom or by video on a screen/laptop. Try to make the extra effort to include those folks, either with eye contact if it's video, or by referencing them in an answer if it's just audio. So tricky!

The upside of interviewing with multiple people is you can be on the lookout for fellow introverts! Sometimes it just helps to know you aren't the only quieter one in the room.

Thea: Is there anything we didn't cover that you would like to mention?

Meredith: I'd just like to add that I think introverts should always try to play to their strengths and be authentic. They don't need to pretend to be an extrovert to get a job. And they don't need to go through the process alone. Job hunting is a great reason to get together with a close friend or two to talk about an interview or to vent about a rejection. Even just a few texts right after an interview with a close friend can help. Definitely try to tap into your network for support!

We Aren't Doomed When It Comes to Job Interviews

I enjoy trips to the dentist more than I enjoy job interviews. But interviews, like dentist visits, are pretty important. Unfortunately, the normal feelings of anxiety that almost everyone feels at an interview can be compounded for an "anxious introvert" because it also includes situations that may not be within our comfort bubble.

First, there's the small talk. Introverts typically dislike small talk, but it is often used in interviews to establish some sort of "normal" connection about ordinary things before the unnatural situation of being asked a series of awkward questions begins. An interviewer may engage in small talk like "how was your trip here" or "it's hot today, isn't it?" in an attempt to put you at ease. Interviews can also be particularly tough for introverts because we aren't as adept at speaking off the cuff as others. Doing an interview requires us to turn on our "extrovert switch," which most of us do not look forward to because it drains our energy.

At first glance, it can seem like we're already doomed before the interview even starts! Of course, the truth is we're just as likely as extroverts to ace an interview if we play to our strengths. And there's one secret weapon in our introvert toolbox that can make all the difference: preparation.

Pivotal Interview Preparing

Yes, extroverts prepare, too, and I've also met introverts who enjoy being spontaneous. However, most introverts are natural preparers, and many of the introverts I've worked with think of preparing as their happy place.

In the past, other people may have even taken advantage of your strength of preparing. During group projects at school or a big project at your previous job, you may have encountered wing-it people who left most of the hard work up to you. Don't discount your innate propensity toward preparation; it is a strength that you can use in the hiring process! Luckily, at job interviews, your hard work and preparation skills will benefit only you.

In the book *What Color Is Your Parachute?: Guide to Rethinking Interviews*, author Richard N. Bolles describes researching, a type of preparation, as "the little secret about interviewing" because "organizations love to be loved."[58] I have a feeling that my natural ability to prepare was a big factor in me getting at least two jobs. For instance, during an interview for an internship at a motion picture production studio, the interviewer asked me why I wanted to work there. When I quoted their mission statement, the interviewer looked at me in surprise. I'm guessing most other interviewees didn't do as much research into the company.

Our prep work can benefit us beyond just understanding the company's values. Before I go into an interview, I take a look at the actual building on Google Maps and what the surrounding area is like. I also scroll around and try to assess the parking situation (if I'm arriving by car). Essentially, I try to reduce surprises and any unnecessary confusion that might arise on the day of the interview. I'm pretty sure my Google Maps fanaticism even led to landing me a job once! I was set to attend an interview for an assistant at a lawyer's office, so I googled the location. The office was down an alley packed with other businesses, and the numbering of the shops was pretty strange. It took me something like ten minutes of searching the area on Google Maps before I finally figured out where my interview would take place. At the start of the interview, the lawyer asked, "Did you find this place okay?" I said I did and that I had checked it out on Google Maps first. She told me that she constantly received calls from people who were trying to locate the office for the first time and were lost. After the interview, I only had to wait a few hours before I got the call from the lawyer—I'd gotten the job! While her question about finding the place may have been intended as standard small talk, it turned out to be an excellent opportunity to show her that I am organized and prepared.

When it comes to preparing, don't stop at internet research. You should also plan your outfit, print out your resume, and take care of everything else days ahead of time. If you're new to job hunting or if it's been a while, practice your answers to standard interview questions and to job-specific questions that you believe will come up. Once you feel like you have a decent grasp of your answers, enlist the help of a friend or family member and give them a list of ten interview questions to ask you. Either in person or through a video program like Skype, rehearse your answers. Then, go back and choose two of the questions that were the hardest for you to answer. Have your friend repeatedly ask you those two questions until you can answer them in a way that feels natural. That way, you'll leave the mock interview feeling positive instead of ending with a that-was-horrible-and-I'm-going-to-bomb-the-interview feeling. If you don't have anyone you can ask for help, record yourself asking those interview questions on your computer or phone, then pretend like you're in the interview by playing back the recording, clicking pause after each question, and saying your answer.

And be sure to have time set aside on your calendar to gain energy before the interview. Can you move around meetings or reschedule social engagements so you can relax and recharge the day before and the day of the interview?

Tips for Managing Introverts

Are you currently running a job search? Certain introverts can find the modern job interview process challenging, and many aspects of the interview may be testing for qualities that aren't needed for the job. How many times does a software engineer have to verbally think on their feet for one hour straight while answering questions like "Where do you see yourself in five years?"

Take some time to consider the ways you can even the playing field between introverted and extroverted job applicants. For instance, what about supplying each interviewee with the questions ahead of time?

If you're doing a daylong interview, make sure you give the interviewee a chance to take several long breaks throughout the day. Many daylong interviews require that the interviewee eat lunch with their prospective coworkers, denying the prospective employee that chance to get a moment to connect with their thoughts and regroup. You may think that eating lunch with prospective coworkers is a good opportunity to see how they can blend into the company culture, but how often are you going to require that employee to be in an unusual and stressful situation and "on" for four hours prior to socializing during lunch? What's tested during an interview can be very different from the day-to-day activities of the job.

If you're doing a group interview, your purpose may be to test who can command a room, be persuasive, and work well in a team, but you may instead be testing for who can talk the loudest or who doesn't mind talking over everyone else.

Here are a few questions you can ask yourself if you want to create an interview process that will help you find the best employee versus the most extroverted employee:

- What was the former interview process actually testing?
- How can I use the new interview process to uncover what I actually want to learn about the applicants?

- Is there a way I can run this interview so it's less stressful for introverts and extroverts?
- Are there misconceptions about introverts that I'm carrying into the interview?

Once you identify the purpose of an interview and its structure to suit that purpose, it will be easier to find a new employee who will truly thrive in that job, instead of just finding someone who can interview well.

Remember Your Superpowers

You have a number of strengths that will help you ace the interview. Remember your top three introvert superpowers from Chapter I? Here they are:

- Our energy is created internally.
- We think before acting.
- We have superior listening skills.

These are all excellent skills to bring to an interview. For one, you're not looking to make friends in this interview; you're looking to convey your competence and excitement for the job. You've done plenty of preparation and are ready to wow the interviewer with your knowledge of the company. You're also at this interview to listen deeply—to understand the questions and answer appropriately, instead of just saying a bunch of words that mean nothing, like politicians who never answer questions directly. You're going to need to use that listening skill of yours to actually answer the question they asked, and not just listen for certain keywords so you can say a carefully rehearsed answer that may not fit the question.

If you're a nonstop nervous talker like Marla from earlier in the book, you might want to allow yourself time to pause for a second before you answer an interview question. Don't beat yourself up; it's good to pause. That short moment of silence might seem a lot longer to you, since you're hopped up on adrenaline, but remember that to the interviewers, it'll seem like a normal break.

State the facts confidently—your strengths, your skills, and what you can bring to the table. Your aim here isn't to convince your interviewee that you're an extrovert; it's to provide them with all the information they need to decide if you will be the best candidate for that job. Without that information, they won't be able to discover the best candidate, so being humble in a job interview or withholding information will not help anyone.

You're Also Interviewing Them

Assuming you have some economic wiggle room and don't have to take the first job that you're offered, if you're facing some anxiety before going into the interview, tell yourself that you are interviewing the company as much as they are interviewing you! After all, you do not want to be working somewhere that will be a bad fit for you. And even if you are in a tight spot and may not have the freedom to pass on an offer, you should still try to keep to this "I'm interviewing them, too" mantra. It will help you stay calmer and project confidence.

A few things to look for when interviewing the company:

- What do they seem the most concerned with during the interview?
- How are they treating you during the interview?
- Do their values seem aligned with yours?

- Are their concepts of work-life balance aligned with yours?
- What is the environment or layout of the office building like—does everyone have their own private office or are coworkers crammed into a deafeningly loud open office?
- Are the interviewers asking inappropriate questions or giving you an awkward vibe? There are plenty of unskilled managers out there, and you may not want to work for them.

While you're interviewing them, you need to determine for yourself: is this a place where I want to work, will I mostly be doing the work I want to do, and are these people with whom I want to work? Your answers to these questions will help you decide if you're considering a job that will drain your introvert energy, and whether the job will give you the feelings of satisfaction necessary to believe the drain is worthwhile.

A job can bring you energy and satisfaction, or it can take those things away. You have the power to interview your prospective employers and make a decision that honors who you are.

Nervous Is Normal, and Excitement Is Excellent

If you find yourself feeling a little nervous as you're on your way to the interview, try to reframe your nervousness as excitement.

Research has found that the simple trick of reframing the interview as something that is actually not that scary is more effective than attempting to suppress anxiety or not letting your anxiety bubble to the surface.[59] Building on this finding, an interesting study by Alison Wood Brooks from Harvard Business

School found that "reappraising anxiety as excitement increased subjective feelings of excitement." If you try this reframe, you may still feel anxious, but by also becoming excited, you can view the interview more as an opportunity rather than something that's scary. Brooks's study went on to suggest that "advising employees to say 'I am excited' before important performance tasks or simply encouraging them to 'get excited' may increase their confidence, improve performance, and boost beliefs in their ability to perform well in the future."[60]

So before you walk into that interview room, while you're in your car or on the bus, start reminding yourself that nervous is normal, but excitement is excellent. That feeling you might have in your stomach could be excitement about the possibilities that lie ahead!

Extreme Anxiety and How It Affects Interviews

I have experienced firsthand how extreme anxiety, when not reframed with the feeling of excitement, can get in the way of doing well in an interview. Many years ago, I had decided that I wanted to be a high school college counselor who would guide teenagers on their path toward attending university. I had done the informational interviews, taken a UCLA course in college counseling, and interned as a college counselor at a high school. Now, it was time to find a paying job related to the field. The first job interview I landed in that field wasn't for a college counseling job; it was for a position in the admissions office of a trade school. It wasn't exactly the perfect job, but it was certainly a step in the right direction. I was eager to start this career, and I really wanted to ace the interview . . .

Well, the interview was a disaster. I was very, very nervous. The little voice in my head that was repeating "don't screw this up" was shouting too loudly during the interview for me to think properly, and I struggled to think of decent answers to the interview questions. I was asked the very standard question: "Why do you want to work here?" I told them that I wanted to work at a public college so I could eventually work at a high school as a college counselor. When the interviewer said, "But this isn't a public college, this is a trade school," the only response I could think of was "I know." I don't think I have to tell you that I didn't get the job.

What I know now, that I didn't know then, is that there is a pattern to the job interviews I aced—practically every time I thought there was no point in going to the interview because I believed I wouldn't get the job, I got the job. And practically every time I went in afraid that I would screw up a big opportunity, I didn't get the job. Take the internship at the production studio I mentioned earlier. When I went into the interview, I had doubted that I could pass off as someone cool enough to get an internship at a celebrity's motion picture production studio. But I got the internship. Then there was that time I assumed there would be other applicants much more qualified to work at a lawyer's office than me. But I got that job, too. When I thought about this pattern a little more, I realized I had had a similar experience with my SATs (the college prep exams in the US)—I received my best score when I had taken the test dead tired and had assumed I would bomb it.

Finally, I realized my anxiety was a form of self-sabotage. When I expected to bomb something, I wasn't nervous, and because I wasn't nervous I could think clearly and act confidently. But whenever I wanted something badly, the pressure and anxiety mounted to the point where I didn't know how to manage it.

Not every introvert struggles with anxiety, and not every introvert will see the same pattern I do (for some, it might be the other way around). But for a number of us, anxiety is like an Olympic sport that we've been practicing daily, since we were children. To friends and family, our anxiety and feats of imagination might even be impressive—and not in a good way.

Combating Interview Anxiety with Non-Attachment

When I finally noticed the self-sabotaging effect that the pressure of "doing well in an interview" was having on me, I realized I could help my chances of getting a job by pretending to not actually care whether I got it. This is a delicate balance—being serious enough to convey to your interviewers that you want the position and doing plenty of preparation, but also being nonchalant enough with yourself to realize that in the grand scheme of life, one interview doesn't really matter. If you've received one invitation to an interview, there's another company out there that's also going to send you an invite; you just don't know about it yet.

I later found out that people have been practicing a purer form of this technique for millennia. Buddhism calls this concept, which exists in many other Eastern religions, *non-attachment*. To quote the Dalai Lama: "Attachment is the origin, the root of suffering; hence it is the cause of suffering."[61]

Frankly, whenever I practice non-attachment, I often feel guilty. The American subculture I grew up in equated striving with success. To be a productive member of society, you must prove your worth and always be striving for something more—you have to always be hustling. But I'd like to call that out as a potentially harmful way of thinking. Just like the cultural misconception that extroversion is "better" than introversion, the concept of always hustling may have negative consequences for the many people who don't fit that always-hustling mold.

You may also want to practice non-attachment in other aspects of the workplace, from dealing with toxic workplace cliques (at least until you get another job someplace else) to asking for a raise.

Using Non-Attachment During the Job-hunting Process

In *101 Small Rules for a Big Job Search*, author Tony Beshara, owner of Babich & Associates, the oldest placement and recruitment service in Texas, points out that job hunting is a process. "You *can't* control getting a job offer," Beshara writes. "You *can* control the right steps it takes to get a job."[62] He also points out that this concept is applicable to many other situations, from running a business to sports. UCLA basketball coach John Wooden teaches, "If you manage the process, you don't have to worry about the score."[63]

The truth is, you can't actually control other people. You also can't control what people think of you, and you can't control whether someone will hire you. What you *can* control is your own actions and reactions.

There are aspects of the job search that may not feel natural to us introverts. But you have innate skills and talents that can help you through this process. You got this. Now go out there and get hired!

"Being an introvert means I am usually the least threatening person in the room, which typically leads to colleagues confiding in me. Also, when I raise a question in meetings, it usually gets heard and discussed as I am not one to typically say something unless it's critical."

—Andy, pediatric audiologist

VI.

KEYS TO COMMUNICATION

You may have heard the phrase "Communication is the bedrock of any relationship" in the context of romantic relationships. But, of course, communication is also vital in all other important relationships in our lives, including our work connections. In this chapter, we'll examine our built-in communication strengths, like listening, and we'll discuss solutions for possible areas of improvement, such as the dreaded "speaking up" in meetings.

Our Listening Superpower

As we discussed in Chapter II, listening *is* a strength. It's a strength that forms the bedrock of communication. Without listening, there is no communication, only noise. And we now live in a world filled with noise. The noise of the modern age ranges from the ding of an email notification to the visual clutter of uninteresting memes on social media. Even emotional noise is now commonplace. Ugly and divisive comments spewed by politicians and comments that might have been discussed for days in newspapers a decade ago are barely noticed now, or at least they are noticed for maybe fifteen minutes until the next insensitive comment by a public figure.

In such a noisy, crowded, lonely world, listening is a superpower. Listening, and paying attention, is now one of the most powerful things someone can give to another person. Listening has always been important, but now it's one of the most valuable currencies.

Strengthening Your Listening Superpower

When I trained to become a life coach, I learned that my desire to solve my clients' problems often meant that I was listening specifically for clues that would help me find solutions; I was not listening deeply to the person in front of me in an attempt to truly understand them.

Do you suspect that you can become better at listening? The following exercise will help you hone your listening skills. When I first I did this exercise, it blew my mind. Hopefully, you'll find it as enlightening as I did.

Step 1: Find an extrovert friend or family member, or a fellow introvert who is a patient person. Explain to them that they will have to talk out loud to you for ten straight minutes, with no interruptions, about a current problem they're experiencing in their life. Let them know that you aren't allowed to say anything back and that you'll be listening to them the entire time with your back turned.

Step 2: Set a timer for ten minutes.

Step 3: Turn away from them, start the timer, and inform your friend that they can start talking. Then, just listen.

Many introverts are taught to fit into the extrovert ideal by spending their internal energy actively trying to talk nonstop or to think of questions to ask the other person, instead of just listening. The end result is that they aren't able to truly listen because they're too busy trying to think of what to say next. But, as I hope you'll discover when you do this exercise, one of the magical things about truly listening is that questions will often naturally pop up in your mind without you having to make any extra effort.

While you are listening to your friend, don't try to actively think of solutions to their problems or force a question into your thoughts. Just listen and be curious.

Curiosity, which children have so much of, is ingrained in all of us. And yet it's very possible that during your formative years you attended a school that taught you that the key to success is memorization, not curiosity. When you let go of trying to fit the extrovert bias that speaking is king, let go of an education system that stamped out curiosity, and let your natural state of listening and openness take over, you'll find the right balance between listening and speaking. It's never too late to hone your listening superpower.

How to Use the Art of Listening in the Workplace

If you're speaking with your boss, don't use up your mental energy trying to think of something—anything—constructive to say or ask. Instead, use your mental energy to listen. If a coworker starts talking to you to get something off their chest, activate your natural listening. You don't have to talk to show that you hear them. Often, someone just wants to hear a sympathetic "Oh, I'm so sorry" and to be heard.

In situations where a give-and-take of conversation is expected, such as a casual workplace conversation or a meet-and-greet at a networking event, you might find that you listened deeply but still can't think of any follow-up questions to keep the conversation going. When this happens, a default easy response I always use is, "And why is that?" You can also use "And what else?" or "Was that always the case?" What are some authentic-feeling, catch-all questions you can deploy to keep a natural flow of conversation? While introverts tend to struggle with thinking on the spot, we do best with preparation beforehand, so I suggest you create and practice five go-to conversation continuers.

We'll talk more about conversation starters and continuers in Chapter VII.

Can You Email Me Instead?

Phone-phobia is real. Although few people have an actual diagnosable phobia of telephones, speaking to a live person over the telephone is still a nightmare that many introverts will do their best to avoid. Just text me, please.

Phones tend to be our least favorite method of communication. A phone conversation can have the same pressure as an in-person conversation—you have to respond on the go with very little opportunity to ponder and think about your response, meaning any pause for thinking seems magnified. And unlike text-based communication on social media or via messaging, you can't just decide you're done with the conversation and get up and walk away.

Unlike in-person conversations, there is also the added complication of being unable to see the other person's body language, making it hard to tell if someone is joking or angry. If you're an INFJ or ISFJ on the Myers–Briggs Type Indicator, or if you're an HSP (Highly Sensitive Person) who is sensitive to other people's emotions, this inability to read someone's body language may be unsettling to you. Plus, they can't see you, either, so a silent nod will get you nowhere.

I used to *hate* talking on the phone. I would have rather spent half an hour trying to find a bit of information off a website than spend five minutes calling someone to get my answer.

Can you relate?

What changed my relationship with phone conversations was simply repeated exposure. After becoming a life coach and doing coaching over the phone and on video calls, I've learned to no longer dread this method of communication. While I certainly don't love phone calls now, I can at least tolerate them. In psychotherapy, the act of reducing anxiety by repeatedly being exposed to the anxious situation in a systematic way, while also applying relaxation techniques, is called *exposure therapy*. If you have a phobia or intense fear, you should seek the help of a therapist. But with smaller inconveniences, such as disliking phone calls, sometimes repeatedly just doing that thing that scares you can help reduce anxiety over time.

If becoming more comfortable with phone calls is something that is important to you, I suggest you start by simply having more phone calls—whether it's for work or for personal errands. Instead of making a doctor's appointment online, spend the extra ten minutes calling instead. Instead of ordering pizza through an app, call in your order. You could also start calling your distant relatives to chat . . . just kidding! That might be too much.

Start with doing easy calls more frequently, ones that don't feel very scary, and develop relaxation techniques to help you become comfortable with them. Techniques could include deep breathing and visualizations—visualizing that the calls will go well. For instance, many of my clients who want to become more comfortable with sales calls find it helpful to simply imagine a successful call before they pick up the phone.

Here's what else changed when I started doing frequent long coaching calls:

- I have become a little more comfortable with inter-rupting. I used to struggle with assertiveness, and it was hard for me to interrupt someone in person. On phone calls, there's an added difficulty because it's not always obvious if someone has finished talking. But after accidentally interrupting my clients many times, purposefully interrupting people has now become a little easier!

- I have become a better listener. Since I can't see the person's body language, listening deeply for emo-tional cues becomes much more important.

- I have become more forgiving with myself, after hav-ing made mistakes while speaking on the phone. For instance, I was once coaching a client when the line became very quiet. As a coach, I was trained to wait for silences (something that goes against the must-fill-quiet-spaces concept in American popular culture), but this silence went on for a while. "Are you still there?" I asked. She responded, "Yes, I'm just crying." I was horrified that I had interrupted an emotional moment (she had had an important realization and was overwhelmed). Luckily, the world didn't come to an end when I made this mistake. She didn't demand that we never speak again, and she continued to have important realizations as my client.

- Now that I'm used to phone calls, I will now just call someone if I think it will save me a decent chunk of time.

In other words, my unofficial exposure therapy worked, and I've gone on to successfully use this repeated-exposure technique on some of my other mild anxiety-producing situations, such as doing presentations.

And one last quick tip: if you're nervous when talking on the phone, try pretending to be someone else, like a celebrity or a fictional character. If you don't have enough courage to speak as yourself, sometimes it helps to borrow someone else's personality. Extroverted online influencer Gary Vaynerchuk once shared that when he does one-minute Instagram videos, he uses the rhythm and intensity of the old-school wrestler Randy "Macho Man" Savage.[64] Even extroverts benefit from borrowing someone else's style on occasion! Which confident person can you embody the next time you need to pick up a phone?

Big Talk vs. Small Talk

You're waiting in line at the grocery store when the person standing in front of you turns around and asks, "What do you think happens to people when they die?" How would you react? You might be afraid that they're a murderer or maybe a salesperson trying to sell you life insurance. Unfortunately (for introverts), small talk is often the necessary bridge one must walk over before jumping into deeper topics, especially when interacting with strangers.

One of the most common things I hear from fellow introverts is that we hate small talk. Small talk feels painful for us. Unlike extroverts, engaging in conversation does not boost our energy; to make things worse, small talk drains our energy and doesn't even give us any nourishing food for thought. *What is the point?* an introvert might ask.

Human beings are social animals. Traditionally, we've had more chances for survival by living in a community that pooled its resources and looked after one another. Many primates groom each other to strengthen social bonds—this is called *social grooming*— but for us human primates it's generally inappropriate for adults to comb each other's hair at work as a team-building exercise! Instead, we have small talk. Small talk isn't a failure to exchange meaningful information or ideas; it's a non-threatening way to discover points of connection. When someone says, "Beautiful day today, isn't it?" they are searching for a point of connection, perhaps one where both of you are uplifted by the weather.

Some extroverts are satisfied with a surface level of communication; however, introverts often want to dig deeper to approach big talk. And the way to access that deeper point of connection is by wading through the shallow surface-level small talk first.

Jessica Pan, the author of the book *Sorry I'm Late, I Didn't Want to Come: One Introvert's Year of Saying Yes* and one of the guests on my podcast *Introverts Talking Business*, conducted an experiment where she spent a year "extroverting." On the podcast, I asked her what she learned about transitioning from small talk to deep talk. "If you are willing to go there," she said, "most people will leap into the deep talk with you as long as you're an authentically interested person who isn't just being totally nosy."[65] But to get to deep talk, you often have to make the first move. Jessica writes, "Not only do you have to be a bit vulnerable *and* a bit ballsy to ask the questions in the first place, but also you're asking whomever you're speaking with to be the same: open up, take your hand, and embrace the depths."[66]

If you want to transition someone from small talk to big talk, I believe the conversation should hit two points:

- You need to show them that they can trust you with their deep, more intimate thoughts. You can do this by sharing something personal or vulnerable with them first. You don't even have to share your darkest secrets; it can be as random as "You know, most people love cheesecake, but I don't."

- Discovering a common interest will create another point of connection. If you hit on a topic that naturally interests them, they're more likely to want to continue the conversation and go deeper. But be prepared to do some small talk to discover that shared interest. I've actually seen two people bond over disliking cheesecake—once they found out that they had this in common, it was as if they had noticed each other for the first time even though they had previously met on many occasions.

It may seem annoying to have to make small talk with our coworkers, but it's like brushing your teeth: while you probably don't love doing it, it's worth the effort in the long run—and it's easy to turn into a habit.

Nervous Is Normal in Public Speaking

The last time you had to speak in front of a group, did you feel like you wanted to literally be anywhere else but there? To quote a line from the TV show *Seinfeld*: "You're better off in the casket than doing the eulogy."[67]

You're not alone. Even famous singers like Adele[68] and iconic actors like Laurence Olivier[69] have had stage fright. In fact, more people fear public speaking than death![70] Luckily, there are certain measures you can take to make public speaking a little less intimidating, and one of those measures is reframing.

Most people consider "public speaking" to mean any sort of presentation in front of a large group of people. While the thought of public speaking in front of a large crowd can be scary, what if you reframe public speaking as something you've been doing on a smaller scale your whole life? The definition of *public* is "of or relating to people in general,"[71] so what if you expand that concept of "people in general" to "any two people or more"? You've probably been able to confidently communicate your thoughts to two people or more at some point in your life without feeling really self-conscious. That counts. Perhaps you've confidently delivered a "speech" in front of a group of fast-food workers about how you'd like your fries extra crispy. Of course, a prepared speech delivered in front of your coworkers or conference attendees is a bit different than ordering fries. But whatever the circumstance, know that in the past you've done some version of speaking to multiple people; you just have to take it to the next level now.

When some of the most powerful speakers deliver presentations, they sound as if they are talking to individuals. I remember the first time I watched Sir Ken Robinson's TED talk entitled

"Do schools 'kill creativity'?" Robinson wasn't going for bubbly or intense energy. He wasn't trying to impress anyone with hype. He didn't even seem as if he were trying to establish himself as an expert. He was just a person up on that stage sharing a compelling story and a point of view that he was passionate about. And even though I was on my computer watching him through a screen, I could tell he wasn't just addressing the audience as a whole. I saw him lock eyes with individuals, at times talking just to that one person. In a way, it felt like he was just talking to me, too.

When you're talking to a room full of people, it helps to tell yourself that you're just talking to a room of individuals. You're actually having a one-to-one conversation, but with multiple people at the same time, and without anyone interrupting you. And you're talking to individuals who would probably feel just like you if they were in your shoes.

The 4 Ps of Public Speaking Success

To conquer your public speaking anxiety, remember the "4 Ps of Public Speaking Success":

- Purpose
- Plan
- Practice
- Prepare

Let's look at each of these in more detail.

1. Purpose

Having a reason you're doing public speaking, a clear *why*, can help you tap into your innate bravery. When someone is excited about a project, they're more likely to *want* to work on it; however, dreading that thing often leads to procrastination, which just adds to the anxiety. So, start your public speaking game plan by creating both an internal and external purpose. Remember that extroverts are generally more excited than introverts about anticipating rewards and having external incentives. So instead of relying on just an external reason for why you want to do public speaking, like raising your profile so you can get a pay raise, think also of an internal reason; for example, "I want to prove to myself that I can get up in front of people and present."

After you find your *why*, take a step back. You also don't want to create unnecessary anxiety because you feel like all the stakes are riding on this presentation. Your entire life's happiness is rarely going to hinge on one event.

In summary, tap into why you're excited to do this talk, then let go of expectations.

2. Plan

Equally as important as the personal reason for doing the talk is your audience's reason for attending the talk. Your audience forms the foundation of your plan.

If you're speaking at a conference, your talk is not about you. If you're giving a presentation at work, your presentation is not about you. Your talk is *always* about your audience. A lesson I learned in coaching school is that everyone is wandering around listening to the radio station WIIFM—What's In It For Me? (Granted, this analogy worked better a few years ago when everyone still listened to radio stations.) In other words, your audience has a specific reason why they are listening to you, and they want to hear a talk that is geared toward that reason, so the first part of planning a talk is to think about how your presentation will benefit your audience.

For instance, say you're a software developer, and you're planning on doing two talks next month about a big project that's nearing completion. You'll be giving one talk at a software development conference, and one talk to the general public. The foundation of your plan for both talks will have to be different. The talk to the general public shouldn't contain too much industry-specific jargon since the audience probably won't be familiar enough with the basic concepts of software development to understand a description of the minutiae of the software or how you solved that bug. Instead, they want to know about how the program itself is going to make their lives easier or better.

On the other hand, if you're giving a talk at a software development conference, you can assume that the audience has at least a basic shared knowledge of software design, so you can use more jargon and go into technical detail about the actual project. Your audience will probably be more interested in how you solved problems in developing the software so they can apply those lessons to their own software development.

The following questions will help you glean insights into your audience so you can build the talk around their needs:

- Why is the audience attending the talk?
- What does the audience want to get out of my talk?
- How can I help them reach that goal?

After you understand what your audience wants, create an overall approach for the talk. Is the purpose of the talk to educate, convince, or entertain?

Combine what your audience wants with your approach to create a thesis for your talk. Now, you're ready to write it! First, start with an outline, and then flesh out the outline until you have the talk written.

3. Practice

Most introverts excel when they have adequate time to practice. Ideally, you'll have prepared for your talk far ahead of schedule and with plenty of time to spare: you'll have finished writing the speech, given yourself plenty of time to memorize it, and made space in your schedule to practice it in front of others.

While you'll want to memorize your talk, you don't want to *sound* like you've memorized it. Instead, you'll want to memorize it until you know it by heart, so that when you deliver it, it feels natural. When Beyoncé gets up on stage to sing "Single Ladies," she doesn't have to consciously access her memory to bring up the lyrics; they just come naturally to her because she knows them by heart. Similarly, by the time you give your talk, you should know your speech intimately.

If your presentation or talk is one that you do frequently, you may not need to set aside too much time to practice. But if this talk is new to you, you definitely do not want to wait until the last moment to rehearse it. Nancy Duarte, a writer, speaker, and CEO, gave an eighteen-minute TEDx Talk and wrote in a blog post that she practiced her talk for roughly eighteen hours.[72] Wow! You may not need to spend that much time, but do embrace the idea of practice. Practicing is an introvert strength!

Once you know your talk well, start testing it out with an audience. Remember that it's okay to take small steps; they are still steps! You may want to start out by doing your presentation in front of a stuffed animal or pet—you won't feel judged, and you won't receive constructive criticism! You can even find an image of an audience on Google and practice in front of that until you're ready to practice in front of a real person. Once you give your talk to your dog or parakeet, move on to family or friends.

Keep practicing, and eventually you'll get to a point where the talk sounds natural. It's like when you learn a new language—at first, you're constantly having to stop and search your memory for the right word, but soon the new language should just flow and you shouldn't have to translate between your native language and the new language. That's what you want to do with your presentation. (And fortunately, it won't involve learning eight thousand new words.)

4. Prepare

Prepare everything ahead of time. For instance, a week before the presentation, choose your clothes and research the parking situation if you're going to a new location. You'll want to decide ahead of time when you would have to leave your home to get to the event ahead of schedule. You want to get there early for two reasons: one, rushing out the door would just add to the stress; two, it'll give you time to go somewhere with a bit of privacy, like a corner of the parking lot or the restroom, to reframe your anxiety as excitement.

Music can help transition your mind from nervousness to excitement. What about singing the lyrics from "Eye of the Tiger" to yourself before giving that talk? Use that energy that's telling you to curl up into a little ball and disappear, and instead redirect it into jumping up and down (literally or metaphorically). Which exciting song can you use as your go-to presentation song?

Now that you've created a purpose for the talk, planned for it, practiced it, and prepared yourself, it's time to do the talk! Remember that talking to an audience can be similar to talking to someone one-to-one. After all, a group is just a number of individuals in one space. You'll do great!

Taking Your Public Speaking Skills to the Next Level

If you're ready to take your public speaking skills to the next level, look for a structured environment designed for growth. If you live in a city, you probably have a public speaking support circle near you. One of the biggest speaking circles is the organization Toastmaster, whose entire purpose is to give its members the support, tools, and practice audience needed to become confident as a public speaker. There are thousands of Toastmasters worldwide, and most will allow you to visit as a guest if you want to check them out first.

I used to go to Toastmasters, and I'm not going to pretend like it was the best fun ever. However, there were always nice and supportive people who completely understood why I thought public speaking was scary. Improving their public speaking skills was the reason *they* were there, too! You may be a little intimidated by the scene at first until you realize that everyone is there to improve and some of them have been practicing for years.

If you find that Toastmasters or another public speaking support circle isn't working for you, you don't have to keep going. There are other ways to improve your public speaking skills, assuming that's one of your goals. I quit Toastmasters after a year and ended up practicing my public speaking on Facebook Lives. It ended up working for me because I felt more comfortable being at home, talking to a camera, and envisioning I was talking to only one person (even though anyone can view Facebook Live). Or you could organize your own speaking circle with a few friends or even coworkers.

Practice makes perfect, or at least practice makes better. And we all have to start somewhere.

Taking Part in Meetings

As a young man in England, Mahatma Gandhi served on the Executive Committee of the Vegetarian Society. He attended every single meeting and often tried to gather the courage to speak, but "was at a loss to know how to express myself." And he found that once he did gather the courage to speak, everyone else had moved on to a new topic.[73] Sound familiar?

While Mahatma Gandhi's shyness as a young man made it difficult for him to participate in meetings, even non-shy introverts can struggle to be heard in the workplace. In a society with an extrovert bias, meetings are often structured to value extroverted ways of being while ignoring or devaluing introversion. Classically structured meetings, where people need to assert themselves to be heard and to speak up even if their thoughts aren't fully formed yet, can be a great place to hear the ideas of a non-shy extrovert, but it is an inefficient way to hear an introvert's best ideas. If you're an introvert who is shy, who has a high level of anxiety, who hates interrupting others, and who likes to think through your thoughts before you speak, the standard large company meeting, where everyone fends for themselves and only the loudest get heard, can feel like a nightmare. It could be proof that your company's culture isn't designed to allow you to excel.

I call these loud free-for-all meetings, which include brainstorming sessions, *"Hunger Games" meetings*. If you find difficulty participating in these meetings, please know that you're not the only one who struggles with them. It's not you that's broken; what's broken is a one-size-fits-all company culture that's not designed for your voice to be heard.

Tips for Managing Introverts

I've heard many managers, both introverted and extroverted, wish that they could hear more from their introverted direct reports during meetings.

Introverts are oriented inward, while extroverts are oriented outward. During a meeting when ideas are being floated for the first time, an extrovert will typically talk through their thoughts and "think out loud," while an introvert will do their best thinking internally. If introverts aren't speaking up in meetings, it's likely that the meetings aren't designed to take advantage of their introverted superpowers.

To create meetings where you can hear the best feedback from everyone on the team, make sure you:

- Acknowledge to yourself that it's not the introverts who are at fault; it's the structure of the meetings that should be improved.
- Don't expect introverts to communicate their best feedback or ideas immediately after hearing new information. Circulating the agenda ahead of time, which outlines the issues that will be discussed, will allow reports to start formulating ideas earlier. Use the meeting as a method for communicating ideas, not for thinking of ideas on the spot.
- Or consider conducting the discussion via an instant messenger service like Slack, perhaps

eliminating the need for an in-person meeting altogether.

- If an in-person meeting is necessary, consider having two short meetings on the same subject—an exploratory meeting, and a meeting where decisions are made. The time between the two meetings will allow introverts to process the information presented in the first meeting and then come up with new ideas.
- Ensure that the loudest people in the room don't monopolize the meetings. If the meeting has a hard ending time, consider limiting the amount of time the loudest people have to speak.
- If you notice a report is not speaking up in meetings, have a judgment-free one-to-one conversation with them to learn what *you* can do to support them. Then take the necessary steps to resolve the issues they raised.
- Take steps to communicate that you value their opinions. Don't use the phrase "you're being quiet; what do you think?" Many introverts have been taught that being quiet is a weakness and will view the word *quiet* as a judgment. Instead, use a more encouraging phrase, like "If you have any ideas right now, I would love to hear them."

- Consider scheduling quiet time during the meeting to think and reflect.

- Introverts can be great at summarizing the ideas presented in the meeting and the next action steps. Allow introverts the chance to use this strength and take on the responsibility of summarizing the meeting.

- Value the input from everyone on the team, and watch out for the "loudest = best" bias.

Using the SPARK Method in "Hunger Games" Meetings

In Chapter IV, I shared my SPARK Method for getting through some of the difficult aspects of work. Let's explore how can we use it in "Hunger Games" meetings.

1. **Support.** Support during these stressful meetings can come from a few sources. Thoughtful managers who may not know how to conduct a meeting any other way can still support you if you tell them how. If it's mainly the overwhelm of these loud meetings that get to you, you can request that your manager ask for your opinion at the start of the meeting. If you aren't very assertive, you can ask your manager to occasionally interrupt the shouting match to ask for your thoughts. If you have an ally at work, you can also enlist their help to toss ideas or questions to you. If you frequently find that the ideas you contribute are then repeated

by someone with a louder voice who then pretends it's *their* idea, have an ally in the meeting who can respond to the louder person: "I'm glad you agree with ___'s idea; I think that's a great idea, too, because . . ." Incidentally, depending on the team dynamic and your personality, you may have some success doing this yourself if you respond, "I'm glad you like my idea. To build on what you've added . . ."

2. **Prepare.** Can you get hold of the meeting agenda? If the agenda isn't typically sent out, can you ask for one? If you at least find out the purpose of the meeting ahead of time, you can walk into the meeting with talking points and questions instead of trying to think of something on the spot.

3. **Achievement.** Recall a time when you were heard in a meeting or when you spoke confidently in front of a group. You've done it before; you can do it again.

4. **Release.** If you're an anxious introvert, thinking that "I must talk in this meeting" may raise your anxiety levels, making it more difficult to actually talk. I suggest having firm intentions instead of pressured expectations.

5. **Kickass.** You have unique strengths that you bring to the table. Is there a way to use your Square Peg Advantage—strengths and interests you possess that your coworkers do not—in these meetings? For instance, if most of your coworkers are extroverts who don't like planning, perhaps you can volunteer to create the agendas for the meetings.

By seeking support during meetings, preparing what you want to say ahead of time, remembering that you've been heard in the past, releasing your anxiety and expectations, and focusing on your own strengths, you can start participating in meetings despite the extrovert bias.

Leaning into Meetings

We can also use the Do-It-Scared technique from Chapter IV to help us take part in meetings:

- **Observe** your annoying coworker Donny. Donny regularly suggests ideas that are obviously horrible, but does so with confidence. Donny will talk about nothing for five minutes, and your boss will still say, "Thank you for your input." Donny assumes that everything that comes out of his mouth is amazing and will respond to every opinion as if he expects everyone to care about what he thinks. Well, you may not care what Donny thinks, but your boss seems to like Donny—or at least like his participation in meetings. So why shouldn't you participate, too? Don't worry about becoming like Donny; even with practice, it might take you decades to become as annoying as you fear you will be. I think it's important to observe the level of confidence that Donny has, even if it's unearned, and learn from it. You should be developing an earned confidence and using it in meetings.

  And if Donny is not a good source of inspiration, observe Ethan. You suspect Ethan is an introvert, since he's typically chatting quietly with one person at a time during holiday parties. You've also noticed that he speaks up in meetings without shouting, but his quiet confidence seems to naturally command attention. Use your natural introvert skill of observing to help you understand how to best participate in the team you belong to.

- **Resolve** is the next item on our Do-It-Scared list. Resolve to say something in the first five minutes of the next meeting (do it early so you don't give yourself time to back out).

- **Reframe** the idea of speaking up in meetings as being generous with your thoughts.

- **Dip Your Toe In** and say, "I think that's a good idea, too," if you can't think of a new point of view to add. You don't have to say something earthshattering at every meeting.

- **Jump In**, and at the next meeting, plan to say something that you have already prepared beforehand (try to get that agenda ahead of time).

If you take these tips to heart and practice, taking part in meetings will get easier, I promise!

Additional Tips for "Hunger Games" Meetings

The SPARK Method and Do-It-Scared techniques are just the tip of the iceberg. Try these additional tips for participating in meetings:

1. Flip the "extrovert switch." As we discussed in Chapter IV, you may find that putting on certain

"extroverted" behaviors is like flipping a hidden switch in the back of your mind. Try to have some sort of external signal to help you flip the switch in meetings. You can flip it while you're getting up and walking to the meeting room with your "walk of power." Or, flip the switch right when you sit down. You may want to experiment with what helps you step into your extroverted side (Carl Jung, who popularized the terms *introverted* and *extraverted*, believed everyone has both sides in them). For me, sometimes sitting up straighter or putting on a big smile is what helps me flip the switch. Sometimes it's singing a hard rock song from the eighties, like "Eye of the Tiger." Once you find those triggers, create rules for yourself. For instance: "walking into the meeting room" = "normal self"; "sitting down in meeting room" = "sitting on the edge of my seat and becoming the 'extroverted' introvert who can command an entire room."

2. If you hate interrupting people, try using your hand and arm instead of your voice to indicate that you want to speak next. I have a soft voice, so my arm basically does the interruption for me. This technique can help whether you want to interrupt or be the next person to speak. I've found that one of the keys to making this work is not to raise my hand sheepishly, as if I am afraid of interrupting (which I am, but my arm doesn't need to know that!). Instead, I motion my hand a little toward the center

of the table, as if I'm reaching in to participate. This movement also feels less awkward to me; I'm not raising my hand upward as if I'm in school again. Don't let your brain override your arm and tell you your voice isn't as important as everyone else's in that room! Let your arm assume that you have the right to speak next.

3. If the arm thing is too weird for you, try clearing your throat. I've actually heard this technique happen during presidential primary debates—even well-seasoned speakers use it! Or, if you want to add to something that someone else is saying, give a verbal noise of agreement or disagreement—*uh-huh* or *uh-uh*—to indicate that you want to speak next, followed by leaning in or moving your hand. Though I've personally never tried this, I've also heard of the trick of loudly dropping something to get everyone's attention before you speak, but that's for more extreme no-one-ever-listens situations.

4. Don't wait until you have a fully formed thought before you start speaking. (This is a huge tip for many introverts!) In "Hunger Games" meetings, you cannot afford to wait until you know what you want to say and how you want to say it. Just like Gandhi experienced, by the time you feel like you can share a fully formed thought, the conversation will have moved to another topic. Instead, if a coworker says something and there's a "spark" in your brain, take it as a sign that you

have something to say on the subject. You may not immediately know the reason you had that gut reaction, but when you feel it come on, just start talking! To give your brain a few extra seconds to gather itself before you present your view, use filler phrases like "I disagree because . . ." And if you don't know how to finish that sentence on the spot, that's okay. A good manager should be fine with you saying, "My gut reaction is yes/no because . . . well, that thought is gone. But can we revisit this at a later meeting? I would like to think more about this."

5. When each person in the room is required to talk, don't anticipate your turn. If we focus on when it's our turn to speak and silently rehearse what we will say while everyone else is speaking during the meeting, our anxiety will just build. Instead, practice listening deeply to everyone around you and trust you will be able to say what you need to when the time comes.

6. Don't wait until your anxiety goes away to speak. It will very likely not go away. Instead, I suggest speaking up before your anxiety builds. If you're in the type of meeting where everyone is providing feedback, aim to be the second person to speak up. It's honestly less scary than freaking out for twenty-five minutes and being the tenth speaker. Also, someone else may have taken your point by then! And why the second speaker and not

the third? Remember: most people don't like public speaking, and especially when in a room of strangers, most people don't want to go first. But once the first person speaks, everyone's courage rises. There's a bit more competition to be the second speaker, and then a lot more competition to be the third. Try to get in early. The last key to thriving with this go-early technique is to release any of the mistakes you may have made while speaking. Let it go and enjoy the fact that you have voiced your opinion and don't have to sit in anxious anticipation any more.

7. What if you're anxious about someone else challenging your statement? Prepare a default response to questions you may not know how to answer. "That's a great question. I'll find out and get back to you on Tuesday about that" sounds much better than "Uh, I don't know."

8. Is there a particular person who always interrupts you? Before the meeting, think of a phrase that will steer the conversation back to what you want to say, perhaps: "Can we go back to discussing ____? I still have a few more ideas I think are important." Knowing that you are prepared to deal with strange questions and interruptions will help you to go along with the flow of the meeting.

Tips for Managing Introverts

Brainstorming sessions, where chaos and shouting reigns, are not the best method for hearing an introvert's best thoughts. And it's not just introverts who can be silent during brainstorming sessions; you also might not hear from HSPs, shy extroverts, or new employees. Fortunately, there are several alternatives to brainstorming you can choose from that will help you hear ideas from everyone on your team.

One of the most common alternatives is *passive brainstorming*, sometimes referred to as *silent brainstorming*. Place a large piece of paper, or a large white board, somewhere that is easily accessible to the team. Communicate to your direct reports that this paper is for brainstorming solutions to a problem. Over the course of five days, allow reports to write their ideas on the paper or board. Then, schedule a meeting to discuss these ideas.

Brainwriting is an alternative method that occurs during a meeting. Participants take a few minutes to write down on an index card a solution to the problem at hand. After everyone is done writing one idea, the index card is passed to the person on their right, who then builds upon it by writing more ideas. After a period of time, say, ten minutes, the cards are collected, read aloud, and discussed.

Duncan Wardle, the former vice president of Innovation & Creativity at the Walt Disney Company, suggests having an *ideation session* instead of a brainstorming session.

Ideation sessions are a lot like brainwriting, only the act of building upon an idea happens verbally. During an ideation session, one participant shares an idea out loud, and then the colleague to their right says, "Yes, and . . ." and proceeds to build upon that idea. They continue to go around the room, with the next colleague to the right building upon the newly combined idea with a "Yes, and . . ." followed by their contribution. I've seen Duncan model this method at a conference, and the idea generated was far more creative than anything that could have been formulated in a classic brainstorming session.[74]

There are so many alternatives to brainstorming sessions out there beyond these three models, which are just the tip of the iceberg. I encourage you to try out one of these alternatives so you can hear ideas from everyone on your team.

Resources for Difficult Conversations

Unfortunately, everyone, introverted or not, will eventually run into "challenging" colleagues or managers. There are so many moving parts that come into play with challenging workplace relationships that whole books have been written to help you out of your situation. Here are just a few of them:

- *Crucial Conversations: Tools for Talking When the Stakes are High* by Kerry Patterson, Joseph Grenny, Ron McMillan, and Al Switzler is a classic for a reason. It's especially effective for introverts because it draws on our introverted strength of preparation in order to get you ready to talk about those tough subjects.

- Gary Seigel's *The Mouth Trap* focuses on honing your workplace communication skills and what to do when you make a mistake—it happens to the best of us!

- If the mere thought of one of your coworkers makes you angry, Katherine Crowley and Kathi Elster's two books *Working for You Isn't Working for Me* or *Working with You is Killing Me* will be helpful, depending on your specific situation. They categorize the different types of problem bosses and coworkers and help you recognize emotional baggage you might be bringing with you to work. They also provide clear and precise tips for moving forward, depending on the type of coworker you're dealing with and your own specific needs.

- Finally, Anne Katherine's *Boundaries Where You End and I Begin: How to Recognize and Set Healthy Boundaries* focuses on family relationships but is a great reference for learning about boundaries in general and their importance.

"The ability to listen and absorb the views and issues of others enables me to get to the root of their concerns. I've had people crying at the end of conversations, just thanking me for listening and saying that they now feel they aren't alone."

—Donna, store colleague at a health shop

VII.

SECRETS TO NETWORKING

Effective networking can lead you to a great new career or to a company better suited to your values. It can also help you move up the ladder to a better position in the company where you currently work. According to a study conducted by LinkedIn in 2017, 70 percent of people who had been hired already had a connection at that company![75] And yet, many people (even extroverts!) don't regularly connect with their network. That same study found that 38 percent of respondents had a hard time staying in touch with connections, with 49 percent saying they don't have enough time to devote to networking.

Do take this study with a grain of salt—LinkedIn's users are on the platform to network. Regardless, these statistics seem pretty accurate in my personal experience. In small (e.g. the museum world) or competitive fields (e.g. television) especially, the number of people hired who already know someone at the company is very high.

For introverts, keeping in touch with numerous contacts in order to maintain our networks can seem like inviting rejection, jumping into overwhelm, or taking a big heaping of awkwardness.

Since we have difficulty anticipating rewards, the hard work of keeping in touch with our network may not feel worth it, but I promise you that it will be!

What Ties Us Together

As we mentioned in Chapter V, it's important to have both weak ties and strong ties when you tap into your network to look for a job. To recap: a strong tie is someone you're close to, like a family member, good friend, or coworker on your team. A weak tie is someone you may occasionally interact with but you aren't close to—an acquaintance. Strong ties will work harder to help you, but since most people have far more acquaintances than they have best friends and family, jobs are more likely to be found through weaker ties.[76] This means keeping in contact with weak ties—your acquaintances—is crucial.

I'll tell you a secret. Maintaining contact with a weak tie actually requires much less effort than maintaining contact with a stronger tie; you just need to have an organized system for reaching out to those weaker ties, which we'll discuss later on in this chapter. Weak ties require less effort because there are lower stakes if anything goes wrong. Unlike your strong ties, these people won't expect you to help them plan their wedding, babysit their kid at the last minute, or comfort them after a bad breakup. If it just doesn't work out with a weak tie, you can break off contact without huge negative ramifications.

Start Now, Please

Now is always the perfect time to start a networking habit! I agree with Karen Wickre, author of *Taking the Work out of Networking*:

An Introvert's Guide to Making Connections That Count, who writes, "This is my guiding principle for no-pressure networking: *nurture it before you need it.*"[77] Even if you're well into your career, wouldn't necessarily call yourself *successful* according to your own goals, and have never taken networking seriously, there's still time! There are countless examples of successful people who started their careers later in life or did not see success until they were much further on.

The English actress Dame Judi Dench was once told by a director that she didn't have the face for movies,[78] and she only became a household name in her sixties when she starred as M in the James Bond film *GoldenEye*. Fashion designer Vera Wang didn't start designing bridal dresses until she was forty. And the folk artist Anna Mary Robertson Moses, better known as Grandma Moses, didn't begin her painting career until age seventy-eight. Your idea of success may not be achieving celebrity status, but the lesson is the same—it's okay to start *right now*, whatever your age or experience!

Let's take a look at the Do-It-Scared approach and how we can use it to start networking:

1. **Observe.** How do other people network? There are a variety of techniques—which ones work for you? Gabe, like many of my clients, thought that networking events were the only way to network, and so he was shocked when we came up with a plan for him to network online so he could bypass in-person events. Doing this online gave Gabe more control over how he used his valuable energy (read more about networking online later in this chapter).

Or you might be like my client Sally who excelled in making connections in person through random conversations, like in line at the grocery store. At the "observe" stage, make your best guess as to what networking *your way* looks like. There's no wrong way to do what works for you!

2. **Reframe.** If networking has serious "Gah, do I have to?" connotations for you, rewrite its definition to turn it into something you can either look forward to or at least not totally resist. For example, Susan Cain thinks of going to a party or networking event as looking for "kindred spirits."[79] But maybe you're not looking for kindred spirits, in which case, who are you looking for? Make looking for that type of person into a game. Perhaps you've noticed that you have an easy time talking to someone with a really unusual job or pastime. While you're at a networking event, make it a game to find a person who raises pygmy goats in their backyard or does pirate reenactments on the weekend. Or just look for characters for your next screenplay. There are fascinating people out there that you'll have fun getting to know.

3. **Resolve.** Your brain will try to trick you into playing it safe. Your emotions may tell you that going to, say, a networking event will make you too vulnerable and that you're not up to it. You may come up with "logical" reasons why it doesn't make sense to network right now. But at the point when you

hear (or feel) a little voice saying, "I should just start networking," shout "Okay, go!" and forego all hesitation.

4. **Dip Your Toe In.** If you decide to network by joining Facebook groups, it's totally okay to lurk around for a week to understand the lay of the land before you start posting—just be sure you *do* start posting! Give yourself a time limit—I'd advise less than a week. If you wait longer than that, it will be easy to slip into your comfort zone of just observing. If you decide to go to networking events, attend a smaller one first instead of a two-hundred-person mega event. If you want to start reconnecting with existing connections, it's okay to start with one person the first week, then bump it up to two the following week. There's nothing wrong with starting small as long as it gets you started!

5. **Jump In.** After you've dipped your toe in a few times and gotten used to it—and hopefully realized that networking isn't as horrible as it originally seemed— jump in. Challenge yourself to reach the next level of networking, whatever that looks like for you.

Wherever you are in your career, it's not too late to get started with networking.

Networking in Five Minutes

It's very common to avoid networking because it feels like you don't have the time to get started. You don't need a two-hour chunk of time to grow your network; all you need is five minutes a day. In five minutes, you can:

- Decide if you want to keep track of weak ties through an app, spreadsheet, pen and paper, etc.
- Set up the weak tie tracking system (more on this in a second).
- Reach out and connect with one person.

If you take five minutes a day to reach out to one person, by the end of the week you'll have reached out to seven people! Why not put down this book and reach out to one person right now?

Weak Tie Tracking System

While you could try to remember the names and pertinent information of each of your weak ties, it's much easier if you set up a weak tie tracking system. I recommend that your tracking system include some or all of the following, depending on what's important to you. The most important things to track are starred:

- *Name
- Birthday
- Location
- Spouse's name
- Children's name(s)
- Family information (and updates on the family)
- Pets
- Sports teams
- *Job

- *Employer
- *How you first connected
- Mutual acquaintances
- *Topics of contact
- *Dates of contact (calls, emails, texts, etc.)

The reason why it's important to include a sentence or two about your topics of contact is so that you can keep your conversations fresh in your memory, including whether you've done that person a favor in the past. The dates of contact will help you keep in contact regularly, if that's part of your strategy.

Networking Events *Are* Weird

I was once at a networking event when I noticed that the person next to me was drunk. I thought this was a fascinating decision on her part, and I'm naturally drawn to people who do unexpected things, so I started talking with her. It turns out she was an introvert who was terrified of such events, but her business coach was the event organizer and he expected her to be there.

Drinking is an extreme solution to assuage networking fears, but it also made total sense to me. Isn't this what people do at parties? Even dinner parties serve wine, or so I'm told. There's a reason for this: according to an article by Joshua Gowin in *Psychology Today*, when blood alcohol levels rise, "drinkers report increases in elation, excitement, and extroversion, with simultaneous decreases in fatigue, restlessness, depression, and tension."[80] It would seem that even the extroverts who drink at parties feel they need the liquid courage to get themselves to the next level.

I'm convinced that we humans, introvert and extrovert, are a self-conscious species who generally aren't used to being around tons of strangers. The anthropologist Robin Dunbar theorized that humans are only comfortable with sustaining 150 stable relationships at one time[81]—these are the people we keep in touch with and think about, not the total number of people we know. This number, by the way, is close to the median number of Facebook friends—two hundred.[82]

So, the next time you walk into a networking event or a party full of strangers, remember that almost everyone else in the room is in the same boat. We're probably all thinking, *Where is our tribe of 150? Who are these people? Are they going to kill me?* The truth is, being among a group of strangers *is* weird, and it's natural to feel out of place. While I don't suggest that you actually show up drunk to a networking event, I do suggest taking a healthy dose of self-compassion.

Making Sure You Attend the Event

How do you make sure you take that first step and commit to going to a networking event without backing out? Oh, believe me, I used to back out of things all the time. Then, I read about that study I mentioned in the beginning of the book, regarding the difference between introverts and extroverts when taking Ritalin and how we perceive rewards. In the hours before a networking event, I'm generally not thinking of the "perceived rewards." If I'm having a bad day, my anxiety takes over and I freak out. So, what I do now is I try to put myself in the frame of mind that led me to sign up for the event in the first place, back when the event was so far in the distant future that I wasn't anxious about it.

Now, whenever I consider attending an event and before I sign up, I rate it in my mind. I do this by asking myself how important or fun the event could be. I don't RSVP for anything less than a seven out of ten. After I send in the RSVP, I add the event to my calendar, and here's the important part—I also write down my rating and the reasons for the number. This way, when the time comes to go to the event, I have a reminder, right there in the calendar, of the "reward" I will get by attending.

Try this out yourself. Let's say you see a networking event on Meetup.org, a website for finding and meeting with groups of people near you who share your interests. You have already decided that networking is important for your career and that you want to focus on in-person networking. Normally, you rate most networking events as a six, but this one promises to be a small event, with less chance of you becoming overwhelmed. So you put a "7" on your online calendar and write down the reasons why. When that event comes rolling around and before you're frantically flipping through every excuse you can think of to get out of it, you'll see right there on your calendar why you signed up in the first place. Don't second-guess your original reason; believe it and give that networking event a go!

Thriving at Networking Events

Instead of feeling like you have to be present for the entire duration of a networking event, recall your goal for participating in the first place. Think of it as if you are planning a trip to the gym. Which is better for your health: standing around in the gym for two whole hours worrying about which piece of exercise equipment you're brave enough to go up to and then just giving up; or showing up, running on the treadmill for ten minutes, and then going home?

Your goal is to make great connections, so I'd recommend setting up a quota for yourself. You may even start with a quota of finding just one interesting person to connect to if you're new to networking, and then bumping that number up to two and then three as you get more comfortable with it. What if you've been at the event for over an hour and you just can't find "your people"? Don't make yourself miserable; allow yourself some self-compassion and go home. It's like poker—sometimes you just have to fold so you can play another day.

So how do you show up to any networking event exuding confidence and putting other people at ease? (And without showing them your nerves or that you would rather be at home curled up with the cat?)

1. Don't arrive stressed. That's common sense, right? Except I'm sure many of us are chronically late to events, arriving stressed out because we've had to rush. Plan to walk into the networking event refreshed, not stressed. It might help if you avoid other draining activities the day of or even the day before the event so you can arrive with your introvert batteries full.

2. Arrive early when there are fewer people. If you can't, plan to arrive late. The fewer people there are, the less draining it will be. Arriving early means that everyone you meet will be refreshed and not yet drained. An early arrival also prevents you from building up anxiety beforehand and allowing yourself to talk yourself out of going.

3. Have a quota. You do not have to talk to every single person at that event. Instead, create a quota: how many promising connections will it take for you to feel satisfied? Remember Susan Cain and her "rule of one" for networking—she's not looking to making twenty new connections; she's just looking for a few "kindred spirits."[83] You don't need to talk to everyone there, or even most of the people there.

4. Let go of the pressure. There can be a lot of pressure surrounding networking events—pressure to attend them; pressure to make a good first impression; and pressure to make the event "worth the effort." But as I mentioned in Chapter IV, pressure will just add to stress. Instead, release those expectations on yourself, and adopt an attitude of just showing up to see what happens.

5. Assume people will like you. Walking into a networking event assuming that you're going to stand out like a sore thumb and not be liked is very stressful. You don't need that stress. Until proven otherwise, assume people will take to you.

Our Secret Networking Weapon

Marissa came to me for help because she hated networking events. Instead of walking away with new connections, she walked away wondering what was wrong with her. They seemed like an awkward waste of her time and a complete energy drain. She was an introvert, and she believed that meant networking would always be a struggle for her.

This was not the first time I had heard an introvert say that they were doomed to struggle with networking. And while networking events can *feel* like our worst nightmare, I know we can be great at networking. I delved a little deeper to search for the root of Marissa's problem.

I discovered that Marissa wasn't making lasting connections because she wasn't truly connecting with anyone she had met. There wasn't a single person she "sparked" with, nobody about whom she thought, *Hey, I'd be okay with keeping in touch with them.*

We dived deeper. Why wasn't she feeling a connection with anyone?

It turned out Marissa was trying to compensate for being an introvert by pretending to be an extrovert. That didn't surprise me. As someone living in an extrovert-focused society, she thought that if the person she was speaking to believed she was an introvert, they would think less of her. That was her first mistake. Instead of coming across as genuine, Marissa was pretending to be the person she thought others wanted to talk to. And I'm guessing the people at the networking event could sense that.

Her second mistake was ignoring her introvert strengths and buying into the American cultural myth that speaking is the primary form of connecting. When she focused on speaking, she ignored her innate strength of listening. Speaking, instead of listening, was not working out in her favor. Marissa knew that the people she was interacting with wanted to be heard, but what was holding her back was her belief, her autofill, that the only way she could show she'd heard them was to, ironically, immediately say something else in response. Generally, people don't want to be talked at. Marissa was so busy trying to come up with a response to what the person in front of her was saying that she didn't have the mental capacity to actually hear what they had just said!

I'm guessing her conversations often turned out like this:

Potential connection: "And that's how, even though I've been doing public speaking since I was twelve, I only won the state championship in public speaking last month."

Marissa: "So, have you been doing public speaking for long?"

Listening is a gift. Listening is powerful. Listening can help you create and build connections.

But what about the random person you're talking to at a networking event? How do you stay focused on what they are saying, particularly if the topic doesn't pique your interest right away? Try to stay engaged in a conversation by becoming curious. Be curious about the individual in front of you. What do they love most about being a financial advisor? What got them started in the field? Even if he or she is the third financial advisor you've met, their reasons can't all be the same; everyone is unique.

At networking events, listening is your secret weapon, and curiosity is your fuel.

Finding Other Introverts in the Crowd

To establish common ground, one of things you can ask the person you are speaking to is the obvious question: "Are you an introvert?" Recall that introverts make up over half the global population! Unless you go to an extrovert-only networking event, I think you'll be pleasantly surprised to find out just how many introverts you'll come across. I introduce myself as an introvert coach at networking events and hear many responses along the lines of "I'm an introvert, too!" There are often a *lot* of us at networking events, perhaps because many extroverts don't have the same need as introverts to attend such events.

Here's how I maximize the possibility of locating the introverts in the crowd:

1. Go early. There could be other introverts already in attendance who are hoping to make connections before the crowd starts to become suffocating.

2. Look outside the venue. Is there a person standing near the door checking their phone? They may be an introvert looking to get away from the crowd.

3. Stand in line for food or drinks. Sometimes we get into a line just to get away from the crowd. Standing in line is a perfect opportunity to talk to someone, since you have built-in conversation starters about the food and drink.

4. Check out the periphery of the room. It's likely that other introverts have positioned themselves there so they can observe the room before they jump in, or they're hoping for someone else to make the first move. Think how happy they will be when they learn you're an introvert, too! I'm usually the first person to introduce myself because I like to rescue others from the awkwardness of standing alone.

Networking Online

Fortunately, in-person networking events aren't the only way to expand your network. The rise of social media has brought introverts more opportunities for networking without requiring that we leave the house.

I've met many wonderful like-minded people, including pretty much everyone I interviewed in this book, on social media. Here's the social media story of how I once made a close friend on Twitter. One day, I looked at my list of new followers and discovered that one of them was another introvert-related account—and she also lived in Los Angeles! I tweeted "Hi," and said something about how it was awesome that we were both passionate about helping introverts and based in Los Angeles. I was very surprised when she tweeted back to say she had noticed that, too (I guess she had been too shy to say hi first), and asked if I would like to meet up in person. I hesitantly agreed. She turned out not to be a serial killer, and we have since become great friends. While I can't guarantee that you'll meet a future good friend on social media, it is a good resource for you to make connections without leaving your home.

I mainly use Facebook and Twitter to find like-minded people for networking, but you can just as easily use Instagram or LinkedIn. (Of course, you should also network with different-minded people to expand your bubble, but when this is the case, the assume-people-will-like-me rule becomes harder.) LinkedIn and Facebook groups are particularly helpful if you wish to flock together with birds of a feather. Back in 2010 there were 620 million Facebook groups,[84] and in 2013 there were 2 million LinkedIn groups,[85] meaning there's almost certainly a group for people who are either in your field, who share your job title, or who have the same specific interests you do.

Just as with in-person networking events, when it comes to online networking, I'm a fan of observing first before diving in. It's perfectly okay to stay silent and observe the scene for a short time while you figure out if this is a group you will feel comfortable in. Many groups allow newbies to post an introduction. If you're up for it, it's a great way to announce your arrival and meet people. You don't even have to create your own post if you don't want to; alternatively, you can observe first, then start commenting on other people's posts to make connections.

A modern rule of networking is to make sure you connect online with someone you only know in person, and, conversely, to make an in-person connection with someone you only know online. Since the internet is crowded with people from all over the world, an actual in-person meeting may not be possible in some situations. However, you can always invite somebody for a "virtual coffee chat." I've done this many times and I think it's a great way to create a deeper connection with an online acquaintance. You can read more about virtual coffee chats in the next section.

Do you attend many conferences? Most big conferences now have their own hashtag, allowing you to find and connect with attendees before the conference even begins. I've preplanned in-person coffee chats or quick-hellos with conference goers who seemed nice or shared a common interest. For instance, on one occasion, someone who was using a conference hashtag mentioned on her Twitter profile that she was a fan of the TV show *Doctor Who*—an immediate reason for me to reach out and say I'd love to meet up during the conference.

One word of warning: sometimes coffee chats turn out to be sales calls. In my personal experience, this seems to be more common with new LinkedIn connections. It might be annoying if you genuinely just want to make a connection, but try to consider it as part of the process of finding like-minded people. Sometimes diamonds are mixed in with the pebbles. If you do happen to end up in one of those sales calls or pitch meetings, consider it practice for when you meet someone you click with.

Virtual Coffee Chats

Curious about virtual coffee chats and not automatically horrified by the idea?

Virtual coffee chats do not actually require you to drink coffee! The phrase is just used to convey that it's an informal meeting with the purpose of getting to know the other person. Your larger goal should be to build a network of people that you would be happy to support, as there is no guarantee they will eventually support you. Meeting with someone virtually allows you to see if there is some sort of connection.

Typically, I conduct my coffee chats as virtual video calls as I find it's easier to get to know the person when we're looking at each other. While I use the website Zoom to hold these virtual chats, you can also use Skype or Facebook Messenger calls.

I recommend keeping the calls pressure free. If you are looking for a new job, don't go into a coffee chat thinking that the person you're talking to needs to offer you a job at the end of it or to send you job leads in order for the chat to be worthwhile.

I always try to end my coffee chats by asking, "How can I support you right now?" And have an answer ready for when they ask you that same question. And if you promised something to the person you're speaking to, don't forget or procrastinate too long before following through with the promise.

Something I've found crucial for networking is the follow-up. Don't make the same mistake I did when I first started, which is to think that just having one random conversation means you now have a new solid contact. Keep in touch after the chat. It's a good idea to email the person soon after to summarize the conversation—not with the goal of recreating what was said word-for-word, but rather leaving things open for future collaboration. For example: "It was wonderful chatting and learning about your interesting career in drought-tolerant landscape design! If I see any job opportunities for you, I will let you know. Please don't hesitate to reach out if there's anything I can do for you."

Occasionally check in with that person. I've personally found this is far more awkward than the actual virtual chat because I have to actively get over my assumption that I would be bothering them. Instead, I focus on the thought that they, like me, probably need a larger network, too. What I try to do is to find an additional reason for contacting them, for instance:

- Share an article about their industry or interest. People send introvert, knitting, and *Doctor Who* articles to me all the time, and I appreciate them reaching out and thinking of me.
- Wish them a happy birthday.
- Send a personal note of congratulations if you see an announcement on LinkedIn, for instance, if they have just celebrated a job anniversary. LinkedIn will often prompt you to send a canned congratulations

message, so any short, personalized note from you will stand out from the crowd. Authentic and kind connection can go a long way.

- If I happen to think about someone randomly, I will often use that as an excuse to email them authentically: "I was just thinking about you and was wondering how that new landscaping tool was going."

There are many websites that can help you keep in touch with contacts, like the CRM (Customer Relationship Management) website Hubspot.com. However, CRMs are often geared toward business owners, so if contact management tools seem too complex for your needs, a simple spreadsheet with the person's name, where and when you first made contact with them, what was discussed in subsequent communications, and any other personal details you don't want to forget can be included in one place. Most email service providers now allow you to delay an email, so you can even automate the checking-in process by writing an email and setting it to be sent out in a month's time (of course, if they happen to check in with you before that, you should schedule that email to go out the following month).

Dos and Don'ts of Networking Online

Dos

Do reach out to strangers and start a conversation.

Do jump into conversations.

Do create your own posts.

Do respond to people's comments on your own posts/tweets.

Do block trolls.

Do have fun!

Don'ts

> Don't criticize the company you work for or your former employers.
>
> Don't criticize your current or former coworkers (I try to take the position of not criticizing anyone online).
>
> Don't say anything you would not say to someone's face.
>
> Don't say anything that could get you fired (sometimes, the safest thing to do is not talk about politics; leave that to your personal or anonymous accounts, etc.).
>
> Don't comment on anyone's appearance (unless you're on a dating site; frankly, even that can be creepy). The rule of thumb is to never compliment someone on something they have little to no control over, even if you think it's true and a compliment. You may be safe commenting on how much you love someone's pink hair or their butterfly tattoo or their checkered suit jacket, but even if you are sincere, you won't know if someone will get a creepy vibe from you.
>
> Don't divulge sensitive secrets about your work.

How to Use Twitter for Networking

Personally, I prefer to use Twitter for networking. While Facebook is all about connecting with others online, many people feel a little weird about friending someone they don't know very well. And since LinkedIn is a networking platform, I've found that people are there mainly to build business leads instead of make mutually beneficial connections; it's just not the place for me.

I see Twitter as a platform that combines the best of Facebook and LinkedIn. I've found that many users on Twitter are open to creating new relationships, and tools like hashtags and Twitter chats make it easy for you to find like-minded people.

Here's how to get started on Twitter:

Step 1: Determine your goal for networking. Are you looking for mentors, career leads, kindred spirits, etc.?

Step 2: Determine the type of person you want to network with, based on your goal.

Step 3: Open an account on Twitter.

Step 4: Fill in your bio. You may want to mention your job title, your industry, and maybe a few words about your interests and passions. Some people tag the company they work for in their bio, but I would be cautious with doing this if you don't want it to seem as if you're talking on behalf of the company. An exception may be if you work for a big company, and mentioning its name would give you automatic clout. Check your company's social media policy first.

Step 5: Write your first tweet. I recommend even something like: "My first Tweet!" You don't need to overthink it.

Step 6: Think of a company, influencer, CEO, or someone else related to your industry. Search for them in the search bar on Twitter. If they seem like an interesting person/entity, follow them.

Step 7: Take a few minutes to look at the bios of other people who are following them. Do any of their followers look interesting? If so, follow those people.

Step 8: A hashtag is a word that is preceded by a hash symbol (#). The hash symbol enables a word to be searchable. Try to enter a hashtag related to your job title or industry, such as #middleschoolteacher, into the search bar. If nobody has used that hashtag, the search results page will show a 0, but if you do see results, spend a few minutes seeing who is tweeting about the subject and decide whether you want to follow them.

Step 9: Use the search bar to search for words in people's bios. For instance, search for "neurobiologist" and then click on *People*. Follow the people who sound interesting.

Step 10: Keep going until you're following at least twenty people!

Step 11: Take a look at your feed. Your feed is where you can see the top tweets by everyone you follow. If you decide that you don't want to follow a certain person after all, unfollowing is as easy as clicking a button. They won't get a notification that you have unfollowed them unless they are using a third-party tool with that capability, which is unlikely.

Step 12: If you see a tweet in your feed that looks interesting, respond to it. Rethink your tweet if it violates any of the Don'ts listed above, but if it passes that test, go ahead and reply. A simple response like "Interesting perspective!" is totally fine. Many introverts think that we should only post something on social media if we experience an earth-shattering event. But recall that small talk is the path to deep talk and deeper connection, so please don't suppress yourself into silence.

Step 13: Pick a Twitter chat—you can find a list of chats at: www.tweetreports.com/twitter-chat-schedule/. Twitter chats are recurring discussions on Twitter about a specific topic that take place at a particular day and time. You participate in Twitter chats by using the hashtag the coordinator has chosen for that chat, and you can read the tweets of everyone else participating by searching for that hashtag. Many Twitter chats are for business owners, but there are some that might be applicable to your job or interests. If you think you've found an interesting Twitter chat, search for the hashtag to make sure the chat is still active since many Twitter chats have been abandoned. If it looks like it is still active, put the Twitter chat on your calendar and then join in! For more information on Twitter chats, follow the Twitter chat queen, Madalyn Sklar, for advice at @MadalynSklar.

Step 14: Tweet me at @introvertology—say hi and let me know you're reading this book!

Step 15: Start tweeting! Share your thoughts with the world. They don't have to be earth-shattering thoughts and observations. Sometimes the most powerful tweets are the every-day tweets, ones that make people realize they aren't alone in this world.

The Horror that Is Work Parties

Although I don't consider myself to be shy, I get very anxious at even just the thought of going to parties or events where the primary purpose is to socialize with people who aren't already my friends. At one long-term temporary job, I so desperately wanted to avoid going to a barbecue that I even told the truth—that barbecues and parties give me intense anxiety.

If your anxiety regarding attending work parties is so intense that it negatively impacts your life, I really suggest going to see either a therapist or a psychiatrist. Some cultures may disregard the importance of mental health and may look down on you seeking help, but that is another mental autofill that serves no purpose and should be rewritten. I honestly think that *everyone* could benefit from a therapist. If you don't have insurance that covers a therapist, do a Google search or ask around—there may be a therapist near you who offers sliding-scale therapy, which means they charge different fees depending on the person's income.

If you don't have anxiety, or your anxiety is manageable enough where it doesn't negatively impact your life, you should attempt to go to work parties when it's really important, such as annual holiday events or parties to celebrate the end of a huge project.

Here's how you can plan to survive a work event:

- Start by choosing which events you want to attend based on your own preferences and what matters to your career. Which is more important to you—the casual barbecue with colleagues, or the official holiday party with everyone in attendance? Which is more worth the effort? Although a chill barbecue may seem more introvert-friendly than a loud party where the entire staff will be present, the barbecue will likely go on for hours, and you might feel pressured to stay in the intimate environment, whereas you can leave anytime you want at most large holiday parties. Or perhaps you're the type of person who would prefer to be outside rather than trapped among a huge crowd of people. You do you!

- Once you've decided on an event, create a goal. Is your primary purpose to make friends at work? To appease your boss? To signal to the people in the office that you want to build relationships with them? Keep this goal in mind, and tailor your experience of the event toward it. For instance, if you'll just be going to the event because your boss expects you to, then make sure your boss sees you—then leave half an hour hour later.

- Always plan ahead of time to avoid rushing. Plan the route you'll take, the clothes you will wear, etc. The worst thing you can do is show up flustered and have to eat the stress sandwich you just made for yourself.

- Have a memorized list of topics of conversation. There's nothing wrong with this, and I suspect many extroverts and charismatic introverts already have topics memorized.

- Plan conversation starters. I've provided plenty of examples to choose from below!

- Plan ways to get from small talk to deep talk.

Choosing Your Conversation Starters

In Chapter I, I shared how the information that introverts take in goes through a neural pathway associated with long-term memory and planning. Instead of just approaching a stranger at a networking event and then trying to think of a conversation starter on the spot, memorize a few ahead of time! Look for three to five conversation starters from the list below, and choose the ones that feel authentic to you.

When looking through the list of conversation starters, you'll notice that some are open-ended questions and others are closed-ended. Closed-ended questions gather facts, while open-ended questions gather explanations. A closed-ended question can be answered with a short response: yes, no, Monday, good, etc. An example of a closed-ended question is: "Have you been to this conference before?" An open-ended question invites an explanation, for example: "What brought you here?" Open-ended questions will turn the conversation into an actual back-and-forth instead of a one-sided interrogation, which is what being bombarded with close-ended questions can feel like. So, when choosing your three to five conversation starters to memorize, make sure to include at least one open-ended question to keep the conversation going.

I often start off with a few closed-ended questions first, particularly if the person I'm talking to seems shy, and then I ask open-ended questions once we get going. I feel that starting with an open-ended question immediately puts pressure on them to carry the conversation. Starting with an open-ended question will also require the other person to come up with a thought-based opinion, which might be too much for a first exchange with a stranger. Make it easy for them! For example:

- Start with this: "How's the [food they just tried]?"
  This close-ended question is a pretty good starter—their taste buds will provide an easy answer for them.

- But not this: "What's the best food you've tried all night?" This requires them to think through everything they've had so far, weigh their options, and perhaps even weigh the politics of who might have made the food. Save this one for later in the conversation when you have already been talking about food for a while. Then, you can even follow that up with a next question: "What's the best food you've *ever* had?" That will probably lead to deeper discussions of their travels or their childhood.

The List of Conversation Starters

The purpose of these conversation starters is to make a connection between you and another person. If you don't like to talk much yourself, the key is to get the conversation going and then steer it toward a topic that the other person is excited about. They'll do the rest from there.

Parties

- "How do you know [host's name]? How long have you known [host's name]? Where did you meet [host's name]?"
- "I love your [shoes, accessories, outfit, etc.]!" This works best if you're genuine. Again, keep the conversation away from physical attributes, and unless you're on a date, never compliment someone on an element of their physical appearance that they have little control over. Hair can be a minefield, since it's both genetic plus style. If you and the person you're

complimenting have similar hair types and you like the way they've styled theirs, you're probably safe, but otherwise I'd avoid it. Remember, you're there to form a connection, not to point out differences between the two of you.

- "Did you travel far to get here tonight? Was there much traffic?" Depending on the town, this can turn into a whole which-freeway-did-you-take-to-get-here discussion, which can get you a good ten minutes of conversation (if you're in Los Angeles like me!).
- "This food looks good, doesn't it? How are the [one of the foods they've tried]?"

Conferences

- "Have you been to [this conference] before?"
- "Do you know many people here? It's my first time here and I don't know a soul." (If this is true.)
- "Ugh, it's still [time] in my time zone! Did you travel far to get here?"
- "I'm really looking forward to this next talk!" (Be prepared to say why.)
- "Have you had much of a chance to see [the city the conference is in]?"
- "What brought you here?"

Work Parties

Here are conversation starters for when you only sort of know someone.

- "Hi, I'm [your name], I work in [your department]. I don't think we've had much of a chance to talk before."
- "How long have you worked at [name of company?]"
- "They did a great job with the decorations, didn't they?" (Be prepared to back that statement up with what you like about it!)
- "The food looks great, doesn't it?"
- "I normally hate to come to these things, but I'm here because [reason]." (Keep it positive!) You can even explain here that you're an introvert—and remember, we're over 50 percent of the population!

Break Time at Work

- "How was your weekend?" If you can remember what they said last week, ask them about it—they'll feel valued and heard!
- "What are you up to this weekend?"
- "How's [kid's name—or "your kid" if you can't remember!] enjoying the new school year? Does s/he like their teacher? What are they going to be for Halloween? Are they excited about winter/spring/summer break?" (Don't assume they celebrate specific holidays, unless they've already mentioned it to you.)
- "I'm really looking forward to getting home this evening and watching Netflix with my cat!" (But you might not want to say this to your boss!)

- "How's your new puppy? Is he still whining?" People usually *love* talking about their pets.
- "Can you believe we had frost this morning, at this time of year?" Weather is supposedly a "boring" topic of conversation, but, honestly, it affects all of us, and most of the time I have a lot to say about the weather.
- And, if you're really stuck, just make a comment about the day of the week. "Monday, huh?"

From Small Talk to . . .

Being a great conversationalist can come naturally to introverts. However, understanding the flow of conversations in the culture you belong to takes practice for both introverts and extroverts. Some introverts may not need the advice in this section. But some other introverts might not have had enough practice chatting with people, especially if they have grown up being told that they were weird, which caused them to avoid conversations with people for fear of judgment. Remember, you'll get better with practice!

Start small, with easy non-personal questions. It's important to warm up, and let the other person warm up, too! Find a subject that they can talk a lot about, but that also leaves room for opinions, which then opens the conversation for you to respond. When you get a fellow introvert started on a topic they enjoy, they can talk for a long time! (If you see me in person, ask me about introversion or the TV show *Doctor Who!*)

Here's a classic Los Angeles–based example, with someone who's not that chatty:

Did you have to travel far to get here? (An easy question
that's not personal.)

No, only half an hour.

Where are you coming from? (Easy question; only a tiny
bit personal.)

Burbank.

*Oh, Burbank! I live in Eagle Rock, so I use the Burbank air-
port whenever I can.* (Since they revealed something
a little personal, it's fair that you also reveal something about yourself—this will help them come up
with conversation topics, too.)

Yeah, it's a great airport.

Have you lived in Burbank long, then? (Follow-up question to the personal info they revealed.)

About ten years.

So you must have seen a lot of change! (Opportunity for
them to talk about something they know more
about than you.)

Yeah, I remember when . . . (If they still give you a laconic
answer at this point, like "Not really" or "Yeah," they
probably don't feel like talking right now, so say that
it's been great to meet them and that you're going to
get something to eat. If they want to keep talking to
you, they'll come with you.)

Where are you from originally, then?

X city.

Once you've mentioned whether you've ever visited or if you
have any relatives or friends there, you can mention where you're

originally from. Then you can expand on what they just said. *How would you say [their first city] compares to this city? What do you miss the most about it? What don't you miss? What do you think is one thing that [this city] might copy from [that city]? Why's that?* Remember, the most important thing is to really listen since that's one of our introvert strengths, rather than worry about what you're going to say or ask next. Continue to read their body language and gauge their interest in continuing the conversation.

Some special considerations about questions for people who belong to minority groups: unless you've been close friends with this person for a long time, my rule of thumb is: "Would I ask this question of someone who is in the same demographic as me?" Even if you're genuinely curious, your colleague is not there to be the representative for everyone else who's in whatever "other" box you're putting them in. They are an individual and deserve to be treated as such. If you want to know more about Estonian customs from your Estonian colleague, for example, first of all, good for you; and second of all, your local library or even the internet are excellent sources. If and only if your colleague brings up the Estonian-wife-carrying contest, then you are cleared to start asking questions on the subject!

If you're not used to transitioning a conversation from small talk to deep talk, remember that it's a skill, and you'll get better at it the more you practice. Networking can actually be fun if you approach it the right way!

"The introverted strength I use at my nine-to-five job is my ability to observe and process. Thinking scenarios through before making a decision has served me very well."

—Carrie, executive director of a nonprofit organization for children and youth

VIII.

LEADING THE INTROVERT WAY

What's Your Autofill about Leadership?

"Introverts can't be leaders," a person I'm close to once told me. That person knew I was the president of a few clubs in college, that I ran popular social media accounts for introverts, that I got paid to lead workshops and coach introverts, and more. And, that person knew I identified as an introvert. Unfortunately, the autofill that introverts can't be leaders was so strong that it overshadowed the actual proof—that if I wanted to step up and guide people, I could and I would.

In the United States, there is a cultural autofill that all leaders are domineering, charismatic, and bossy extroverts. We know this is far from the truth. Introverts make great leaders in every field and sector. In the tech industry, Steve Wozniak, cofounder of Apple, has implied he's an introvert.[86] In the entertainment industry, Grammy Award–winning singer Lorde is an introvert,[87] while one of the most powerful women in America, Oprah Winfrey, has identified as an introvert.[88] Billionaire Warren Buffett, investor and CEO of Berkshire Hathaway, is often cited as an introvert.[89] I could go on.

But cultural autofills can be so strong that some people will still fail to acknowledge that this is a myth, even if they have proof that the autofill is incorrect. It's not uncommon for someone to flat-out refuse to believe that a person is an introvert simply because they are a leader. Retired US Army major general Heidi Brown has experienced this misconception, and in an interview on National Public Radio, she said, "I'm an introvert by nature, and people would say, 'oh, you're not.'"[90] Because of these prejudices, there are far more introverted leaders out there than most people would believe.

Stereotypes can also lead to self-fulfilling prophecies, and I think this myth that introverts can't be leaders has led to fewer of us being represented in leadership positions—not just in private companies, but also in the current White House. For twenty-eight years, consultant and author Herb Pearce has helped people to understand their personality using two very popular personality assessment tools, Myers-Briggs and Enneagram. In his book *Presidential Profiles: Washington to Trump: Enneagram and Myers-Briggs Perspectives*, Pearce researched each of the forty-four presidents of the United States before guessing their personality based on the data. Interestingly, he found that twenty-three US presidents have been introverts and twenty-one have been extroverts; however, there is a key difference between the personalities of the first ten presidents and the most recent ten. Of the first ten, Pearce believes seven were introverts and three were extroverts, while seven of the most recent presidents are extroverts and three are introverts. This suggests a major shift in American culture regarding the qualities believed necessary to lead the country.

It has been proposed that American culture has changed over time regarding what it values in a citizen's personality. In her book *Quiet*, Susan Cain theorizes that American culture has moved from a "Culture of Character," where honor and dignity are highly regarded, to a "Culture of Personality," which considers gregarious extroversion as the ideal. The good news is that since American culture, as well as other cultures around the world, has shifted before, it can change again. With the increased awareness over the past ten years of our introvert strengths, and the increasing number of celebrities who describe themselves as introverts, I hope we're about to enter a new era where more introverts, as well as the people who make hiring decisions, understand that being a domineering and loud extroverted leader is just one of many leadership styles.

Are Leaders Made or Born?

One of the most harmful theories of leadership is the "Great Man" theory. This theory, which states that great men (i.e., great leaders) are born and not made, was popularized in the nineteenth century by historian and writer Thomas Carlyle, who said, "The history of the world is but the biography of great men." I think this theory is harmful for a few reasons. For one, I believe that effective leaders must possess a number of skills, and that such skills can be learned. If leadership isn't at least partially skills-based, then nobody can take steps to become a better leader. In addition, this theory appears to be reserved only for the people (well, technically only the men during that time, since the contributions of women leaders were often ignored) who have transformed history. This doesn't have to be the case; most people can be leaders even if they don't create an earth-shattering impact.

Often, someone new to leading will think of leadership as a big, complicated, and intimidating role with many moving parts. Actually, it's much simpler than that: a leader is someone who enters a new territory and has at least one other person following after them. If you look into your past, I'm sure you'll find many instances where you were a leader or where you exhibited leadership traits. Perhaps you organized a birthday surprise for a family member or colleague, or set the tone of a meeting, or mediated a disagreement. You did those things by using certain leadership skills. So, whenever you step into a leadership role, know that you aren't starting from scratch.

Another reason I disagree with the "Great Man" theory is that it doesn't take into account the personality of the people who are being led. If you're an introvert who is about to lead a group of proactive employees or volunteers, you're in luck. Adam Grant of the University of Pennsylvania's Wharton School of Management, and his colleagues Francesca Gino and David A. Hofmann, studied a national pizza delivery company to discover if leadership style affected results. They found that for employees who were passive and not very proactive, an extroverted leadership style was associated with 16 percent *higher* profits! However, in franchises where workers were proactive and offered suggestions, extroverted leadership resulted in 14 percent *lower* profits.[91] This study shows not only that different leadership styles exist, but also that the extroverted leadership style associated with commanding the center of attention and dominating discussions is not inherently better than an introverted style of leadership.

What Makes A Great Leader?

There are probably tens of thousands of books and studies written and conducted that seek to answer the question: "What makes a great leader?" In the well-known business book *Good to Great*, author Jim Collins presents a theory that runs counter to the theories of extrovert-biased cultures. Collins and his teamed analyzed companies that appeared on the Fortune 500 in the years 1965 to 1995. They found eleven companies that exhibited a "good to great" quality, and these companies had a fifteen-year stock slump (at or below the general stock market), followed by a transition period, and then by fifteen years of soaring stocks that grew at least three times as fast as the market average. His team then compared these good-to-great companies to the Fortune 500 companies that did not have a fifteen-year stock slump followed by fifteen years of soaring stocks. They found that the "good to great" companies shared a number of qualities, including what Collins calls "Level 5 Leadership." These leaders weren't the archetypal leader with charismatic and loud characteristics; instead, they were "self-effacing, quiet, reserved, even shy."[92]

There's a myth, particularly in the technology sector, that great leaders are charismatic asses, as Steve Jobs supposedly was. But this runs counter to Collins's findings. Instead, great leaders are "seemingly ordinary people quietly producing extraordinary results."[93] They are also people who are "fanatically driven, infected with an incurable need to produce *results*."[94] Their lack of extroversion wasn't a detriment to their ability to turn a good business into a great one; in fact, perhaps it was their introversion and reserved nature that made them great leaders.

Your Natural Leadership Abilities

Let's take a look at our top three introverted strengths and how these play into how we lead.

1. Our energy is created internally. Yes, this does run counter to one of the primary purposes of leadership in the workplace, which is interacting with reports. But there are benefits to being an introverted leader. For instance, we're not going to distract employees by trying to get our extroverted energy needs met by them. How many people do you know who complain about not being able to get their work done because their boss just keeps talking? I've been to many meetings that have gone over the allocated time because the manager shared a personal story that had no relevance to what the team was doing, which resulted in inefficiencies.

2. We think before acting. Have you had a manager who acted prematurely or constantly changed their mind? By thinking before we act, or before we require our reports to act, we can save our team a lot of time, energy, and frustration instead of sending them off down the wrong path only to yank them back and send them in a different direction. Trust is crucial, and your reports are more likely to trust a leader who shows that they value their team's time and resources.

3. We have superior listening skills. As proactive listeners, when we read (or rather, listen) between the lines of what reports are saying, we are much

more likely to catch and resolve issues in the workplace that may not be reported. Through our listening and observation skills, and ability to empathize with our fellow introverts, we will be more likely to retain all our employees.

Creating A New Leadership Autofill

If you're an introvert hoping to step into a leadership role but are struggling to understand how you'll succeed as a leader, here's how to create a new autofill that will convince you that introverts (including you) can make excellent managers!

- Acknowledge that introverts are amazing leaders.
- Pick an introverted leader mentioned in this book, or who you've discovered online, as inspiration and proof that we make great leaders.
- Create a visual cue or reminder of introverted leadership for yourself. This could be printing out a photo of your favorite introverted leader, like Mahatma Gandhi or Eleanor Roosevelt, or even a fictional introverted leader like Kermit the Frog. You can also save their picture as the background to your computer or phone. Repeated exposure will help you reprogram your brain with the new reality.
- Determine what your unique, positive leadership traits are. If you're not good at self-assessment and frequently put yourself down, ask someone close to you to evaluate your attributes. Remember, you're not looking for extrovert traits here; you're looking for introvert traits that can be used in leadership.

For instance, perhaps you're good at synthesizing information—gathering data from many sources in order to see the complete picture. Or you may be excellent at observation and are able to look at your reports and analyze their gifts and talents. Perhaps you don't like tooting your own horn but love shining the spotlight on the people in your team and advocating for their work needs. Maybe you think through new ideas thoroughly before presenting them to your team, bolstering your reports' trust in the direction you're taking the project. Plus, your listening skills can help you gather information from all of your reports to make an informed decision.

Although extroverts may be thought of as the stereotypical leader, introverts can, and do, make amazing leaders. We all have different strengths that can help us lead an effective team.

Share Your Goals

If you want to become a CEO, manager, team leader, or project lead, start documenting your moments of leadership in or out (for instance, volunteer work) of the workplace. Then, schedule a meeting with your manager to discuss what you need to do to reach your goals. Do not just assume that they already know you want a promotion or more responsibility.

> A good manager is invested in seeing you succeed, but first they need to know what success looks like for you.

Take the initiative, and start seeing yourself as a leader.

Expert Introvert Corner with Alex Carter, Leadership Coach for Introverts

Alex Carter is a coach specializing in helping introverts find their authentic leadership style. Alex knows what it's like to be unexpectedly tapped for leadership, to doubt her abilities, and to finally come out the other end proud of her introvert power. I love that she is now using what she has learned to help introverts embrace their inner leadership potential.

Thea: What led you to becoming a leadership coach for introverts?

Alex: There were a couple of reasons. First, there was my own experience as an introvert in a leadership role. When I was first promoted, I felt like someone had made a mistake. I wasn't the stereotypical leader—I have social skills, but I am not charismatic and certainly not "bold." I couldn't make a snap decision if my life depended on it. I was fortunate enough to find a coach who helped me understand that I could be an effective leader by exercising my own unique strengths. I learned there are different ways to be a leader.

The second reason is that once I started looking at the work world through an introvert-extrovert cultural lens, I realized how disadvantaged introverts are. Most workplaces are geared toward extroverts, which leaves half the population feeling uncomfortable at best and nervous wrecks at worst. (I think Susan Cain's book *Quiet* had just come out when I came to this conclusion.) I figured that if I could benefit from coaching, other introverts could as well. And, in addition to making a difference to one individual person, my work with that person could in turn make a bigger difference in various organizations.

Thea: Why do you think introverts often don't think of themselves as leaders?

Alex: One: I think there's a strong stereotype in our culture about what or who a leader is. We see it in everything, from presidential politics to boardrooms. Leaders "should be" dynamic, sociable, etc. Think of politicians kissing babies, displaying oratorical skills, etc.

Two: people who are quieter or slower to speak don't "make an impression" on their higher-ups.

Three: people who thrive in extrovert cultures tend to hire people who are like them in important ways. Extroverts hire extroverts, just as men tend to hire men, and white people hire white people. These trends are changing as we realize the social and business costs. I have hope that we can get the culture to realize that introverts "hold up half the sky."

Thea: You mentioned that people who are quieter or slower to speak don't "make an impression" on their higher-ups. Is there anything an introvert can do about this?

Alex: Absolutely. If you want to move into management or leadership, don't keep it to yourself.
Talk with your supervisor about it. Your supervisor can offer tips on what will help you move up.
There are other specific things you can do to be
seen or heard by your superiors. For example, if
you're having trouble forming thoughts or being
heard in a meeting, it's okay to send a follow-up
email to the meeting convener to offer your
perspective.

Thea: What qualities make introverts natural leaders?

Alex: The three introvert qualities that make for great
leadership are listening well, connecting with people one on one, and thinking deeply. It's becoming
clearer and clearer that empathy and trust are
among the most important elements of effective
leadership. Empathy is when you care about people, and trust is when your coworkers know that
you care about them and will go to bat for them.
The great news for introverts is that empathy and
trust are best developed by (a) listening to people,
and (b) meaningful one-on-one conversations.
This is solidly in the introvert wheelhouse.

Listening is also important when making
decisions—you have to listen to different perspectives, tradeoffs, etc. Then, you have to think
deeply about these issues as decisions are made.
Introverts rarely make rash decisions.

Thea: What would you say to an introvert who is considering a managerial position but who is worried about the energy drain and exhaustion?

Alex: This is a real concern. Let's not minimize it. Introverts are, by definition, drained by lots of "peopling." It's important to learn to manage your energy. First, get good sleep. To me, sleep is the bedrock of all self-care. My ability to deal with people is in direct proportion to the quality and quantity of sleep I get.

Second, eat what's good for you, never go to work hungry, and never skip lunch.

Third, find a physical practice that works for you. Some people like to run or bike. Others do quieter bodywork like yoga or tai chi.

Fourth, schedule time every day to be alone and do what recharges you. I had one client who frequently ate lunch in her car in a nearby park so that she could have alone time and listen to music. Some people use the commute to and from work as solo time—they read or listen to a good book or just process the day on the way home. These four elements will set you up to be resilient at work.

And as a leader, there are ways to structure your day to support your energy needs. First, it is permissible to close your door. Second, schedule in "thinking time"—and keep the appointments. Third, schedule in your meetings, if you must have them, whenever your energy for others is recharged and high enough.

Board of Advisors

You don't have to go through the leadership process alone. In Chapter IV, I mentioned that mentorships can be beneficial for your career; this is especially true if you're stepping into a leadership role for the first time. Mentors can come in many forms, like paid coaches, formal unpaid partnerships, or informal guides.

In the book *Pivot*, Jenny Blake explains that an unpaid professional mentorship and support relationship can begin with a "one-off mentorship," a conversation where someone you admire meets with you for a quick fifteen- to twenty-minute conversation and provides you with advice. If the one-off mentorship blooms, these mentors may become part of your "board of advisors," people you consult with regularly and look toward for advice and ideas.[95] Blake describes this board of advisors as helpful to the growth of a business, but the same applies to an individual's career growth. Seeking help and guidance from someone with more leadership experience can accelerate your progress.

You can turn to your board of advisors for advice like:
- How to run an effective meeting
- Improving your time management
- How to handle difficult reports
- Improving communication skills
- How to hire or fire someone
- Tips on introvert energy management

Which leaders can you connect with and ask for a quick chat about a specific problem? They may say no, but they may also say yes.

Closing the Communication Chasm with Extroverted Reports

Perhaps life would be easier if we all had the same personality! Maybe there wouldn't be as many miscommunications. But that's not the world we live in. Instead, we live in a society where literally everyone is different. And one of the biggest differences I've found are the ones between introverts and extroverts.

As we talked about in Chapter I, introverts gain energy by going inward, while extroverts gain energy by interacting with others. Neither way of being is the best or the right way. Unfortunately, these fundamental differences can lead to clashing styles of communicating.

A potential chasm between you and your extroverted reports comes down to communication preferences. Extroverts think as they talk, while introverts think *and then* talk. It may feel like there's no way to bridge this gap, but a little patience and understanding goes a long way.

When you're working with an extroverted report, at first it may seem as if they just like the sound of their own voice, but the reality is they're most probably trying to come to a conclusion the best way they know how. Know that they're not likely to hit upon a fully formed opinion within their first sentence, and give them space to talk through their ideas. Since extroverts think as they talk, they also like to get opinions from a variety of sources, making formal or informal meetings helpful to them. Consider giving your extroverted reports group work so they have people to bounce their ideas off of.

You can also hold open-office times. Your extroverted reports might prefer to talk things through in person, while your introverted reports might prefer to email you questions. I've seen many introvert managers announce they will hold open-office times, but then they don't follow through. If you do intend to commit to setting open-office times, get clear with yourself on why such meetings are important. If you find that your extrovert reports like to drop in unannounced to chat, firmly communicate your boundaries to them.

If we want the best out of your reports, I believe it's necessary to adapt to their personality, not require them to adapt to yours. In the book *The Mouth Trap*, extrovert Gary Seigel points out that "Every day, in every office, people want to be themselves. The idea of customizing a message for someone else seems time-consuming and overwhelming. . . . Nevertheless, that's what we have to do in order to create rapport."[96]

There may be big differences between introverts and extroverts, but we all have a shared humanity. Don't be intimidated; you have what it takes to communicate effectively with your extroverted reports.

Stepping into the Three Roles of Entrepreneurship

Going into entrepreneurship can be a freeing option for many introverts. But before you quit your day job to become an entrepreneur, you should first know what you're getting into. Entrepreneurship requires many different skills, such as strategic thinking, discipline, patience, multitasking skills, and more. And unless you have the ability to immediately hire staff, you'll likely be filling every role in the company yourself.

A common frustration with new entrepreneurs is that while they're often really good at creating what they're trying to sell, running a business is a lot more than just creating a product or service. In the book *E-Myth Revisited: Why Most Small Businesses Don't Work and What to Do About It*, author Michael Gerber explains how every business must have three people—an Entrepreneur, a Manager, and a Technician. The Entrepreneur does the strategic dreaming about the business. The Manager creates the systems. And the Technician does the actual work—the creation of the product or the service.

So, while you may be really good at what you do (a Technician), you also need the systems in place to effectively run your business, and you also need the vision of what the business should look like and what you need to do next to grow it. Entrepreneurship may seem freeing, and many people think of entrepreneurs as having their days filled with only the things they love to do. However, the truth is that's most likely going to be far from the case when you're first starting out. In the early stages of your business, you'll most likely have to be the entrepreneur, manager, and technician all rolled into one.

The main takeaway is for you not to be dissuaded from running your own business, but to be prepared for the many hats you'll have to wear until you can hire help.

Exploring Business Ideas

How do you start building a business? First, you start with an idea, or two. If you have an idea, but you're not sure if it's too weird or unusual, I suggest you check out fellow introvert Chris Guillebeau's book *100 Side Hustles: Unexpected Ideas for Making Extra Money Without Quitting Your Day Job* for inspiration. The book features a hundred unique businesses, ranging from organizing a karaoke league to leading bicycle tours around the Canadian wine region.

Once you have your idea, it's time to do research to translate it into a viable business. It's easy to have a great idea, one that your family and friends will applaud. However, the problem is your family and friends should not be your business's only target market; they may not even be the right audience who would naturally buy the product. If you want to learn more about how to do research into the viability of a business, check out fellow introvert Pat Flynn's book *Will It Fly?: How to Test Your Next Business Idea So You Don't Waste Your Time and Money*. Another great book on this subject is another Chris Guillebeau book, *Side Hustle: From Idea to Income in 27 Days*.

Once you've determined that your idea has potential, that people want your product or service, and that they are willing to buy it, please don't quit your day job yet! I've seen many cases where people have an idea, manage to sell a few products or services, then quit their day job, only to then experience a dry spell. You don't want to be stuck in this position because it creates a lot of pressure on you to sell to make ends meet, and your customers will be able to sense that desperation, even if you're selling something online. Instead, I recommend working on the business on evenings and weekends outside of your main job until you have proof that the business can support you in the long haul.

To be an effective leader, introverts need inner drive, a willingness to learn new skills, and knowledge of their introvert strengths. And as leaders like Mahatma Gandhi prove, you can even learn to lead if you're a shy introvert. Whether introverts want to become leaders in their workplace, in their community, or through entrepreneurship, they do have what it takes!

CONCLUSION

"Everyone shines, given the right lighting."

—Susan Cain

In this "introvert positive" age of an increasing acceptance of introverts and our skills, we are in a unique time in history to thrive in the workplace. Sure, lingering cultural autofills will mean that not everyone will always understand us, but a crucial first step is to take the time to understand ourselves. We know that while we might have to bend ourselves in a few ways to accommodate the current cultural bias toward extroversion, we do not have to break. As introverts, we have valuable strengths that no one can take away, and we can use those strengths to thrive in our careers. The world is lucky to have you here, and it can sure use your skills, your wisdom, and your introversion.

ACKNOWLEDGMENTS

It's not an exaggeration to say that thousands of people have helped make this book possible. Thank you to everyone who have followed me over the years at Introverts Everywhere and Introvertology, and who let me know that my voice matters and that we introverts matter. Thank you to all of my coaching clients, former and current, who have allowed me to be part of your journey; I am honored.

Thank you to my supportive family who did a lot of rah-rah-ing: Jessamy, David, Suzi, Sarah, Darby, Frannie, Joe, Max, Megan, Noah, and Lily. Special thanks to my wife Jessamy who proofread countless paragraphs and rewrote quite a few sentences when I had a deadline but couldn't think coherently anymore, and who morally supported me during my near-daily "what in the world am I doing" existential crises. To Noah, Max, and Dad for your help in research. To Mom for sharing her workplace wisdom.

Thank you to everyone at Skyhorse Publishing. Special thanks to Kim Lim, my editor, for your patience and for turning a bunch of jumbled words into something that makes sense—and for letting me write this book.

Thank you to all of the experts I interviewed: Beth Cubbage, Lynn Dutrow, Patrick L. Kerwin, Beth Gea, Meredith Tseu, Alex Carter.

I can't thank everyone who has supported this book's journey, but a special thank you to Carrie Skinn-McEachran, Lisa Avebury, José Ignacio Sierra, Gina Ruiz, Brenda Miller, Michael Lao, Julia Barnickle, Alice Southern, Donna Anne, Stacey Webb Horn, Jon McClain, Angelica Winton, Cortney Brandenburg, Tania-Briannë Fox, Nancy Kalina Gómez Edelstein, Gwen Freeman, Tony Dee, Valente Molinar, Eva Lujan, and Andy Lau. Apologies if you expected to be on this list but aren't; it's late at night and I'm surprised my brain is working at all.

Thank you to Alison Carminke, Tracy Ann Guillet, and Peter Gavel for looking after my Facebook group "Introverted Entrepreneurs Community" when everything got to be a little too much for me to juggle.

To the people who joined "Thea's writing a book," you followed along on my journey, and you sent me so many words of encouragement—thank you.

And finally, to every introvert around the globe, thank you for being you.

Endnotes

1   Martin J. L. Boult, Richard C. Thompson, and Nancy A. Schaubhut, "Well-being and MBTI® Personality Type in the Workplace: an International Comparison," CPP The Myers-Briggs Company, 8, accessed January 10, 2020, http://people. themyersbriggs.com/rs/788-YSM-155/images/Well-being%20 WP%20FINAL.pdf.

2   Mohandas K. Gandhi, *Autobiography: The Story of My Experiments with Truth* (Mineola: Dover Press, 1983), 82.

3   Laurie Helgoe, *Introvert Power: Why Your Inner Life Is Your Hidden Strength* (Naperville, Illinois: Sourcebooks, 2008), xxi.

4   Isabel Briggs Myers et al., *MBTI® Manual for the Global Step I™ and Step II™ Assessments*, 4th ed. (The Myers-Briggs Company, 2018), 156.

5   Susan Cain, *Quiet: The Power of Introverts in a World That Can't Stop Talking* (New York: Broadway Paperbacks, 2012, 2013), 21.

6   Marti Olsen Laney, *The Introvert Advantage: How Quiet People Can Thrive in an Extrovert World* (New York: Workman Publishing, 2002), 43.

7   Nur Syahirah Roslan, Lila IznitaIzhar, Ibrahima Faye, Mohamad Naufal Mohamad Saad, Subarna Sivapalan, and Mohammad Abdul Rahman, "Review of EEG and ERP studies of extraversion personality for baseline and cognitive tasks," *Personality and Individual Differences* 119 (December 2017): 323–332, https://doi.org/10.1016/j.paid.2017.07.040.

8   Luke D. Smillie et al, "Do extraverts get more bang for the buck? Refining the affective-reactivity hypothesis of extraversion," *Journal of Personality and Social Psychology,* 103, no. 2, (2012): 306-326, http://dx.doi.org/10.1037/a0028372.

9   Jenn Granneman, *The Secret Lives of Introverts: Inside Our Hidden World* (New York: Skyhorse Publishing, 2017), 24.

10   Jennifer O. Grimes et al., "Four meanings of introversion: Social, thinking, anxious, and inhibited introversion (January 2011), https://www.researchgate.net/publication/263279416_Four_Meanings_of_Introversion_Social_Thinking_Anxious_and_Inhibited_Introversion.

11   Melissa Dahl, "So Apparently There Are 4 Kinds of Introversion," NY Magazine online, June 25, 2015, https://nymag.com/scienceofus/2015/06/apparently-there-are-four-kinds-of-introversion.html.

12   Angela Hope Murray, *Ayurveda for Dummies* (Chichester: John Wiley & Sons, Ltd), 10.

13   M. M. Pandey et al., "Indian Traditional Ayurvedic System of Medicine and Nutritional Supplementation," *Evidence-Based Complementary and Alternative Medicine*, 2013, Article ID 376327, 12 pages (2013), https://doi.org/10.1155/2013/376327.

14   Sahare Rose Katabi, *Ayurveda (Idiot's Guide)* (Indianapolis: DK Publishing, 2017), 29.

15   Gilbert Childs, *Understand Your Temperament!: A Guide to the Four Temperaments : Choleric, Sanguine, Phlegmatic, Melancholic* (Forest Row: Sophia Books, 2009), 4.

16   Richard I. Evans, *Conversations with Carl Jung and reactions from Ernest Jones* (New York: D. Van Nostrand, 1964), 67.

17   Paul T. Costa, Jr. and Robert R. McCrae, "Four Ways Five Factors are Basic," *Personality and Individual Differences,* 13, no. 6, (June 1992), 653-665, https://doi.org/10.1016/0191-8869(92)90236-I.

18   Karene Booker, "Extroverts have more sensitive brain-reward system," Cornell University, accessed January 27, 2020, https://news.cornell.edu/stories/2013/07/brain-chemistry-plays-role-extroverts.

19   Alike Tellegen, Thomas J. Bouchard, Kimerly J. Wilcox, Nancy L. Segal, David T. Lykken, Stephen Rich, "Personality similarity in twins reared apart and together," *Evolutionary Psychology,* Volume 1, 2003, 94. https://citeseerx.ist.psu.edu/viewdoc/summary?doi=10.1.1.318.4777.

20   Susan Cain, *Quiet: The Power of Introverts in a World That Can't Stop Talking* (New York: Broadway Paperbacks, 2012, 2013), 12.

21   Gil Greengross and Geoffrey F. Miller, "The Big Five personality traits of professional comedians compared to amateur comedians, comedy writers, and college students," *Personality and Individual Differences* 47 (2009): 79-83, https://doi.org/10.1016/j.paid.2009.01.045.

22   Elaine N. Aron, *The Highly Sensitive Person: How to Thrive When the World Overwhelms You* (New York: Broadway Books, 2016), xvii.

23   Aron, *The Highly Sensitive Person: How to Thrive When the World Overwhelms You,* 98.

24   Frederick G. Conrad et al., "Interviewer Speech and the Success of Survey Invitations," *Journal of the Royal Statistical Society,* Series A, 176, Part 1 (2013), 191-210, https://www.jstor.org/stable/pdf/23355183.pdf?seq=1#page_scan_tab_contents.

25   Scott Berry Kaufman, "Will the Real Introverts Please Stand Up," Scientific American Blogs, June 9, 2014, https://blogs.scientificamerican.com/beautiful-minds/will-the-real-introverts-please-stand-up/.

26   Temple Grandin, Temple Grandin website homepage, accessed October 27, 2019, https://www.templegrandin.com.

27   momo, "Q&A with Jennifer Yuh Nelson, Director of 'Kung Fu Panda 3,'" Center for Asian American Media website, January 15, 2016, http://caamedia.org/blog/2016/01/25/qa-with-jennifer-yuh-nelson-director-of-kung-fu-panda-3/.

28   Emmanuel J. Rupia, Sandra A. Binning, Dominique G. Roche, and Weiqun Lu, "Fight-flight or freeze-hide? Personality and metabolic phenotype mediate physiological defence responses in flatfish," *Journal of Animal Ecology* 85, no. 4 (April 2016), https://doi.org/10.1111/1365-2656.12524.

29   Mary E. Oswald, Mathew Singer, and Barrie D. Robison, "The Quantitative Genetic Architecture of the Bold-Shy Continuum in Zebrafish, *Danio rerio,*" *PLoS ONE* 8, no. 7: e68828, July 1, 2013, https://doi.org/10.1371/journal.pone.0068828.

30   Lyudmila Trut, Irina Oskina, and Anastasiya Kharlamova, "Animal Evolution During Domestication: The Domesticated Fox as a Model," *BioEssays* 31, No. 3 (March 2009): 349-360, https://doi.org/10.1002/bies.200800070.

31   David Lambert Lack, *The Life of the Robin, Bird-lovers' manuals* (London: H. F. & G. Witherby Limited, 1943), 145, https://books.google.com/books?id=wZs_AAAAYAAJ.

32   Brian Wansink and Jeffrey Sobal, "Mindless Eating: The 200 Daily Food Decisions We Overlook," *Environment and Behavior* 39, no. 1, (January 1, 2007): 106-123, https://doi.org/10.1177/0013916506295573.

33   Geert Hofstede, "Dimensionalizing Cultures: The Hofstede Model in Context," *Online Readings in Psychology and Culture* 2, no. 1 (2011), https://doi.org/10.9707/2307-0919.1014.

34   Etienne Danchin, Sabine Nöbel, Arnaud Pocheville, Anne-Cecile Dagaeff, Léa Demay, Mathilde Alphand, Sarah Ranty-Roby et al., "Cultural flies: Conformist social learning in fruitflies predicts long-lasting mate-choice traditions," *Science,* 362, no. 6418 (2018): 1025-1030. https://doi.org/10.1126/science.aat1590.

35   Ken Binmore, "How and Why did Fairness Norms Evolve?," in *The Origin of Human Social Institutions, Proceedings of the British Academy, vol. 110,* ed. W. G. Runciman (New York: Oxford University Press, 2001), 149-170.

36   W. G. Runciman, *The Theory of Cultural and Social Selection* (Cambridge: Cambridge University Press, 2009), 23. https://doi.org/10.1017/CBO9780511819889.

37   Twila Tardif et al., "Baby's First 10 Words," *Development Psychology* 44, no. 4 (July 2008): 932, https://doi.org/10.1037/0012-1649.44.4.929.

38   Jennifer Kahnweiler, "Can introverted leaders be assertive?" accessed November 4, 2019, https://jenniferkahnweiler.com/can-introverted-leaders-assertive/.

39   Lewis Carroll, *Alice in Wonderland*. (Urbana, Illinois: Project Gutenberg, 2006), chap. 6, retrieved October 30, 2019, from http://www.gutenberg.org/files/28885/28885-h/28885-h.htm

40   Seth Godin, "Totaled," Seth's Blog, February 25, 2018, https://seths.blog/2018/02/totaled/.

41   Richard Feloni, "A Zappos employee had the company's longest customer-service call at 10 hours, 43 minutes," *Business Insider* website, July 26, 2016, https://www.businessinsider.com/zappos-employee-sets-record-for-longest-customer-service-call-2016-7.

42   Guy Kawasaki, "How to Rock the First 90 Days of a Job," February 21, 2015, https://guykawasaki.com/how-to-rock-the-first-90-days-of-a-job/.

43   Julie Zhuo, *The Making of a Manager: What to Do When Everyone Looks to You* (New York: Portfolio/Penguin, 2019), 134.

44   "Law of Jante," Wikipedia, accessed October 30, 2019, https://en.wikipedia.org/wiki/Law_of_Jante.

45   Herodotus, *The Histories*, 5.92G, trans. A. D. Godley, (Cambridge: Harvard University Press, 1920), accessed January 10, 2020, http://data.perseus.org/citations/urn:cts:greek-Lit:tlg0016.tlg001.perseus-eng1:5.92G

46   Benjamin Franklin, *The Autobiography of Benjamin Franklin,* https://www.varsitytutors.com/earlyamerica/lives-early-america/autobiography-benjamin-franklin/autobiography-benjamin-franklin-chapter-nine.

47   Jon Jecker and David Landy, "Liking a Person as a Function of Doing Him a Favor," *Human Relations* 22, no, 4, (August 1969): 371-378, https://doi.org/10.1177/001872676902200407.

48   "Top Five Regrets of the Dying," *The Guardian* Online, accessed October 30, 2019, https://www.theguardian.com/lifeandstyle/2012/feb/01/top-five-regrets-of-the-dying.

49   Alison Wood Brooks, "Get Excited: Reappraising Pre-Performance Anxiety as Excitement," *Journal of Experimental Psychology: General* 143, No. 3, (2014): 11, https://doi.org/10.1037/a0035325.

50   His Holiness the Dalai Lama and Archbishop Desmond Tutu, with Douglas Abrams, *The Book of Joy: Lasting Happiness in a Changing World* (New York: Avery, 2016), 325.

51   "10 Types of Negative Self-Talk (and How to Correct Them)," Nick Wignall website, July 27, 2018, https://nickwignall.com/negative-self-talk/.

52   "Hedge (linguistics)," Wikipedia, accessed November 18, 2019, https://en.wikipedia.org/wiki/Hedge_(linguistics).

53   Jeremiah Dillon, "Read This Google Email About Time Management Strategy," *Fast Company* website, December 14, 2015, https://www.fastcompany.com/3054571/the-better-time-management-strategy-this-googler-taught-his-coworkers.

54   Bill Taylor, "Why Zappos Pays New Employees to Quit—And You Should Too," *Harvard Business Report* online, May 19, 2008, https://hbr.org/2008/05/why-zappos-pays-new-employees.

55   Laura K. Gee, et al., "Social Networks and Labor Markets: How Strong Ties Relate to Job Finding on Facebook's Social Network," *Journal of Labor Economics* 35, No. 2 (April 2017):485-518, https://doi.org/10.1086/686225.

56   Tara Sophia Mohr, "Why Women Don't Apply for Jobs Unless They're 100% Qualified," *Harvard Business Review* online, August 25, 2014 (accessed November 6, 2019), https://hbr.org/2014/08/why-women-dont-apply-for-jobs-unless-theyre-100-qualified.

57   Stacey Lastoe, "8 Ways You Can Still Land an Interview When You Don't Meet All the Requirements," accessed January 10, 2020, https://www.themuse.com/advice/8-ways-you-can-still-land-an-interview-when-you-dont-meet-all-the-require-ments.

58   Richard N. Bolles, *What Color Is Your Parachute? Guide to Rethinking Interviews*, (New York: Ten Speed Press, 2014), 14.

59   Brooks, "Get Excited," 2.

60   Brooks, "Get Excited," 12.

61   "Buddhist stance on consumer culture," http://blogs.evergreen.edu/daysmore/buddhist-stance-on-consumer-culture/ (accessed November 17, 2019).

62   Tony Beshara, *101 Small Rules for a Big Job Search* (New York: Savio Republic/Post Hill Press, 2017), 7.

63   Tony Beshara, *101 Small Rules for a Big Job Search: New Guidelines for Today's Job Seeker* (Savio Republic, 2017), 6.

64   Gary Vaynerchuk, "Manage Your Time with Accountability & Self Compassion," *The GaryVee Audio Experience,* Podcast audio, May 31, 2019, 11:21, http://askgaryvee.garyvee.libsynpro.com/manage-your-time-with-accountability-self-compassion-wine-pizza-with-dave-east-dj-clue-eytan-sugarman.

65   Jessica Pan, "Extroverting for a Year with Jessica Pan," interview by Thea Orozco, *Introverts Talking Business,* Podcast audio, June 3, 2019, 14:00, https://introvertology.com/podcast/episode42/.

66   Jessica Pan, *Sorry I'm Late, I Didn't Want to Come: One Introvert's Year of Saying Yes* (Kansas City: Andrews McMeel Publishing, 2019), 155.

67   Larry David, "The Pilot (Part 1)," *Seinfeld,* Season 4, Episode 23, NBC, May 20, 1993.

68   Touré, "Adele Opens Up About Her Inspirations, Looks and Stage Fright," *Rolling Stone,* April 28, 2011, https://web.archive.org/web/20190210103457/https://www.rollingstone.com/music/music-news/adele-opens-up-about-her-inspira-tions-looks-and-stage-fright-79626/.

69   Michael Blakemore, "The day Lawrence Olivier got stage fright," *The Guardian,* September 17, 2013, https://www.theguardian.com/books/2013/sep/17/laurence-olivier-national-theatre-blakemore.

70   Karen Dwyer and Marlina Davidson, "Is Public Speaking Really More Feared Than Death?," *Communication Research Reports* 29, No. 2 (2012): 99-107, https://doi.org/10.1080/08824096.2012.667772.

71   *Merriam Webster,* "public," revised October 25, 2019, https://www.merriam-webster.com/dictionary/public.

72   Nancy Duarte, "10 Ways to Prepare for a TED Style Talk," accessed November 17, 2019, https://www.duarte.com/presen-tation-skills-resources/10-ways-to-prepare-for-a-ted-format-talk/.

73   Mahatma Gandhi and Mahadev H. Desai, "XVIII. Shyness My Shield," in *An Autobiography: The Story of My Experiments with Truth* (Boston: Beacon Press, 1993).

74   Duncan Wardle, "How to Harness the Momentum of Your Ideation Sessions," Duncan Wardle website, August 23, 2018, https://duncanwardle.com/how-to-harness-the-momentum-of-your-ideation-sessions.

75   Linkedin Corporate Communications Team, "Eighty percent of professionals consider networking important to career success," Linkedin Newsroom site, June 22, 2017, https://news.linkedin.com/2017/6/eighty-percent-of-professionals-consider-networking-important-to-career-success.

76   Laura K. Gee, Jason Jones, and Moira Burke, "Social Networks and Labor Markets: How Strong Ties Relate to Job Finding on Facebook's Social Network," *Journal of Labor Economics* 35, no. 2 (April 2017): 485-518. https://doi.org/10.1086/686225.

77   Karen Wickre, *Taking The Work Out Of Networking: An Introvert's Guide to Making Connections that Count* (New York: Gallery Books, 2018), 32.

78   "Judi Dench Told She'd Never Be in Movies Because of 'Every Single Thing Wrong with Your Face," Irish Examiner online, March 5, 2015, https://www.irishexaminer.com/breakingnews/entertainment/judi-dench-told-shed-never-be-in-movies-because-of-every-single-thing-wrong-with-your-face-664863.html.

79   "Susan Cain: Networking for Introverts," YouTube video, 22:25, interview by Marie Forleo, November 12, 2013, https://www.youtube.com/watch?v=hcvleuvJD0w.

80   Joshua Gowin, "Your Brain on Alcohol," *Psychology Today*, June 18, 2010, https://www.psychologytoday.com/blog/you-illuminated/201006/your-brain-alcohol.

81   Wikipedia, s.v. "Dunbar's number," accessed November 20, 2019, https://en.wikipedia.org/wiki/Dunbar%27s_number.

82   Aaron Smith, "What People Like and Dislike about Facebook," Pew Research Center Fact Tank, February 3, 2014, https://www.pewresearch.org/fact-tank/2014/02/03/what-people-like-dislike-about-facebook/.

83   "Susan Cain's Conversation Tips for Introverts," interview by Ozan Varol, Next Big Idea Club website, July 29, 2019, https://heleo.com/conversation-susan-cains-conversation-tips-for-introverts/21353/.

84   Nick O'Neill, "Google Now Indexes 620 Million Facebook Groups," *Adweek*, February 1, 2010, https://www.adweek.com/digital/google-now-indexes-620-million-facebook-groups/

85   "2 Million LinkedIn Groups" infographic, *LinkedIn*, August 20, 2013, https://www.slideshare.net/linkedin/linked-in-groups-2013-infographic.

86   Jonathan Vanian, "Apple Co-Founder Steve Wozniak Talks Innovation, Microsoft, and Being Introverted," *Fortune*, April 21, 2017, https://fortune.com/2017/04/21/steve-wozniak-apple-microsoft/.

87   Lisa Robinson, "Yes, Lorde's New Songs Are Definitely About Her Personal Life," *Vanity Fair* website, June 5, 2017, https://www.vanityfair.com/style/2017/06/lorde-melodrama-album.

88   "Oprah and Amy Schumer on Being Secret Introverts," Oprah website, April 27, 2018, http://www.oprah.com/own-supersoulsessions/oprah-and-amy-schumer-on-being-secret-introverts-video_2.

89   Andy Hinds, "Warren Buffett, the World's Richest Introvert," Susan Cain's website, accessed January 10, 2020, https://www.quietrev.com/warren-buffett/.

90   Heidi Brown, "Lonely Club For Women In Top Army Jobs," interview by Rachel Martin, *On The Front Lines: Women In War,* NPR, February 25, 2011, https://www.npr.org/transcripts/134025084/.

91   Adam Grant, Francesca Gino, and David A. Hofmann, "The Hidden Advantages of Quiet Bosses," *Harvard Business Review,* from December 2010 issue, https://hbr.org/2010/12/the-hidden-advantages-of-quiet-bosses.

92   Jim Collins, *Good to Great: Why Some Companies Make the Leap and Others Don't* (New York: Harper Collins, 2001), 12.

93   Collins, *Good to Great,* 28.

94   Collins, *Good to Great,* 30.

95   Jenny Blake, *Pivot: The Only Move That Matters Is Your Next One* (New York: Portfolio/Penguin, 2016), 94-97.

96   Gary Seigel, *The Mouth Trap: Strategies, Tips, and Secrets to Keep Your Foot Out of Your Mouth* (Franklin Lakes: Career Press, 2007), 88.